PICTURING WRIGHT

AN ALBUM FROM FRANK LLOYD WRIGHT'S PHOTOGRAPHER

Pedro E. Guerrero

FOREWORD BY MARTIN FILLER

POMEGRANATE ARTBOOKS ■ SAN FRANCISCO, CALIFORNIA

An Archetype Press Book

Text and photographs copyright © 1994 Pedro E. Guerrero
Foreword copyright © 1994 Martin Filler

Published by Pomegranate Artbooks
Box 6099, Rohnert Park, California 94927-6099

Produced by Archetype Press, Inc., Washington, D.C.
Project Director: Diane Maddex
Art Director: Marc Alain Meadows
Assistant Art Director: Robert L. Wiser
Assistant Editor: Gretchen Smith Mui
Assistant to the Author: Dixie Legler

Library of Congress Cataloging-in-Publication Data
Guerrero, Pedro E.
        Picturing Wright : an album from Frank Lloyd Wright's photographer /
        Pedro E. Guerrero.
                p.   cm.
        Includes index.
        ISBN 1-56640-804-0
        1. Wright, Frank Lloyd, 1867-1959. 2. Architects—United States—
        Biography. 3. Guerrero, Pedro E.—Contributions in architecture.
        I. Title.
        NA737.W7G84   1993
        720'. 92—dc20   93-30120
                                                              CIP

Photographs: page 1, Frank Lloyd Wright demonstrating organic architecture, 1953;
page 2, the architect at the drafting table in his studio at Taliesin, 1947;
page 176, a personal interpretation of the roof of Wright's Unitarian Meeting House
in Madison, Wisconsin, 1953.

10 9 8 7 6 5 4 3 2 1
Printed in Hong Kong

CONTENTS

FOREWORD

By the time Frank Lloyd Wright breathed his last, in the early hours of April 9, 1959, there seemed little doubt that he was the greatest architect the United States had ever produced and perhaps this country's greatest artist in any medium. As Wright himself had been the first to predict, the years since his death have only confirmed that high assessment, as new generations have come to appreciate the universality, timelessness, and continuing pertinence of his architecture.

But so vivid was Wright's presentation of himself, so dominant was his celebrity toward the end of his long, eventful life, that the true character of the man tended to be somewhat obscured by his carefully staged persona. Much in the same way, Wright's publicity-attracting late schemes—from his astonishing Guggenheim Museum to the alarming Mile High skyscraper—overshadowed what we can now see as his most enduring contribution: the almost infinite variety of ways through which Wright showed how we could use the machine to live in fuller harmony with nature.

Wright the Titan ultimately became so fixed in the popular imagination that few recalled him as the unheeded prophet who had wandered in the desert, figuratively and literally, during a crucial phase of modern architecture that inexplicably excluded him. Wright's final emergence from that wasteland and his ascent to the very peak of his creative strength might stand as a metaphor for his fer-

vent belief in the power of regeneration that he learned from his *lieber Meister,* Louis Sullivan (who, alas, did not possess his most famous student's perpetual resilience and constitutional optimism).

The vigor of fresh growth permeates Wright's reputation-reviving schemes of the mid-1930s, which in several respects outstrip even his revolutionary works of the first decade of this century in sheer imaginative audacity. And seen within the larger context of Wright's seventy-year career, those boldly original solutions provide the most convincing evidence of the adaptability of Wright's principles beyond the limitations of mere style.

It was Pedro Guerrero's great good fortune—and ours—that he was present at that unheralded high point in Wright's development. There is as yet no definitive (or even wholly satisfactory) biography of Wright, whose protean personality and staggering accomplishments await the exhaustive study equal to his significance. Until then, we must depend on the individual views of perceptive eyewitnesses. To the short list of the most credible we must now add this memoir by "Pete" Guerrero (as the master himself insisted on calling his most faithful photographer).

Such was the force of Wright's personality that those closest to him have not always been the most reliable commentators, for proximity does not guarantee perspective. Furthermore, Wright at the time of his second coming was

With many of Mr. Wright's projects in the 1950s concentrated in and around New York City, numerous occasions arose to photograph him as he inspected works in progress at various sites, including here at the Usonia homes in Pleasantville, New York in 1952. There always were revisions to be made and challenges posed by unforeseen problems; sometimes he would just simplify a drawing that had a workman confused. A Wright design was never finished—not absolutely—especially if he had a chance to look at it once more.

7

seventy years old, not so much a father figure as a grandfather figure to his devoted disciples. Wright's all-encompassing view of architecture as but one (albeit the most basic) component in a life fully lived required that the building art extend to all realms of human existence and vice versa—hence his conception of the Taliesin Fellowship and its embodiment of the complete commitment to the cause of architecture that Wright demanded.

Whatever the Taliesin Fellowship was later to become, during the decade after its founding in 1932 it was nothing less than Wright's vehicle for personal and professional survival. Following his departure from Oak Park in 1909 (ostensibly to supervise the preparation of the Wasmuth portfolio of his lifework but actually to escape his first wife and children and live with his lover, Mamah Borthwick Cheney), Wright never again found the ready-made constituency for his work that his progressive, sympathetic Chicago-area clientele gave him at the outset of his practice. By the early 1920s and the advent of a new kind of modernism, his lean years had begun.

It might be said that Wright had a head start on the Great Depression a decade before the fact; that national economic crisis, on the heels of his private one, could well have spelled the end of his building career, as it essentially did to those of his like-minded contemporaries Bernard Maybeck and the brothers Greene. But Wright prevailed by returning to his roots at Taliesin in Wisconsin, and once he was thus reestablished he transplanted part of that root system to the surprisingly hospitable soil of the Arizona desert.

It was into the expansive atmosphere of the newly built Taliesin West that the twenty-two-year-old Pedro Guerrero entered in late 1939. Bearing a portfolio of student photographs and hopes of working for the exotic enterprise recently established at Scottsdale (not far from his hometown of Mesa), Guerrero in fact had only a hazy idea of what that calling might entail. But Frank Lloyd Wright—for all of the casualness with which he seems to have appraised and taken on the young aspirant—had known from his days as chief draftsman in the office of Adler and Sullivan how vital pictorial representation of architecture can be. And Wright saw in Guerrero the perfect opportunity to mold an eager, emergent talent to the specific needs of his revitalized firm. Within months of his arrival, Guerrero became the chief visual intermediary between Wright and the architect's eager new audience.

The disparity between Wright's recaptured eminence and Guerrero's initial inexperience did not matter to the elder man as much as did their agreement on the central factors of their common mission: a dedication to the art of architecture and making it understandable to a broad public. From the outset Guerrero showed an immediate, instinctive understanding of Wright's architectural intentions; a cooperative nature open to achieving precise results; an innate feel for the spirit of a place—not just his native terrain but also the locales of other Wright structures across the country; an ability to convey the texture, mass, detail, and substance of Wright's schemes in two-dimensional form; and a desire for continuity that enabled him to work with complete assurance of Wright's expectations despite their divergent paths over two decades.

Soon after he was accepted into the fold at Taliesin West, Guerrero became close enough to watch Wright in many unguarded moments. As his shrewd judgments reveal, this photographer's powers of observation on a personal level are no less acute than those readily discernible in his now-historic pictures. Through his eyes we see Wright not as the autocratic head of a personal fiefdom of serfs (as the communal but hierarchical organization of the Taliesin Fellowship sometimes has been portrayed) but as a man who was genuinely concerned for the welfare of his hard-working charges and who understood their need to stand by their own beliefs, as he had by his.

Nowhere is this clearer than in Guerrero's moving account of the agonizing decision he reached to leave the Fellowship and enlist in the army, following his father's urging that as a Mexican American he must do so to avoid the taint of divided loyalties. But to do so he would be countering Wright's isolationist and pacifist sentiments. Yet when Guerrero finally gathered the courage to tell his mentor that he felt compelled to leave him and take part in a cause that Wright deplored, the architect nevertheless expressed his understanding and support. As a parting gesture, Wright impulsively handed the photographer two hundred dollars, far from a small sum in 1941.

Wright's buoyant temperament surfaces time and again in this account. The architect's seriousness of vocation was absolute, but he never let it interfere with his enjoyment of life. Great music, good food, fine art, and lively companionship were an integral part of the Taliesin experience. The joys of creativity in the widest sense were being taught by Wright just as surely as architecture was. If the tone of the pursuits at the Fellowship now seems somewhat quaintly dated, we must think of Wright as the last leaf of the Aesthetic Movement. And yet his insistence on the wholeness of life and art—omnipresent in his work if only we will see it—reminds us why the fragmentation of American architecture today reflects our social conditions as accurately as Wright's improving approach reflected the reformist aspirations of his time.

Pedro Guerrero's classic photographs are simultaneously documentary and evocative. In several instances they preserve the only visual record we have of Wright's work as it appeared upon completion. There are heroic sun-struck images of daily life and labor at Taliesin West and studies of Taliesin in winter that belie the cameraman's enchantment at witnessing his first snowfall. Wright himself appears in many guises—guru, grand seigneur, gadabout, good old boy, grandpa—and yet whether he was on guard for Guerrero's portrait lens or taken by surprise, he always seems conscious of his role of great man and is playing it (and relishing it) to the hilt.

Although an ardent admirer of the man who transformed his life, Guerrero is no acolyte, and his cumulative depiction of Wright, while fond, is anything but fawning. But Guerrero is correct in seeing that above Wright's quirks and crotchets hovers his largeness of spirit, which allowed him to encompass so much and embrace so many in his work. No wonder that the vast number of celebrated architects since Wright's death seem bereft not so much of his genius as of his generosity.

Lewis Mumford got to the heart of the matter when in 1953 he wrote, "Of the two fundamental Freudian types of personality, the hoarding and the spending kind, one tight and compulsive and the other relaxed and generous, Wright belongs firmly to the second. His expansiveness, his exuberance, his inclination to put both form and function highhandedly at the service of his own singular genius are an essential part of his own inexhaustible creativeness."

Similarly, Pedro Guerrero's openness to the extraordinary access he was given to Wright during his comeback season gives his own work an authenticity and savor as rare in his specialized field as his subject's gifts were in his own. As one turns these pages, filled with visions of high purpose and great beauty, one can almost hear the words of the "Work Song" that Frank Lloyd Wright composed as his personal anthem:

I'll live as I work as I am
No work for fashion in sham
Nor to favor forsworn
Wear mask crest or thorn
My work as befitteth a man
My work
Work that befitteth the man

Martin Filler

PREFACE

Frank Lloyd Wright changed the course of my life forever—at age twenty-two it was impossible to imagine just how much. As it turned out for me, as for so many others, his influence has been manifested almost daily. Even today, more than fifty years later, I am engaged in the preparation of books, articles, and exhibitions commemorating and celebrating his life, his contributions to the world of architecture, the generous gift of his privacy and time to his apprentices, his genial company to his many friends, and his genius for yet another generation to discover. I was part of his world at a very early age, and yet it truly seems as if it were only yesterday. But I did not exactly arrive at Mr. Wright's doorstep in a basket with a note pinned to my blanket. I had skills yet to be fully developed, and he was the instrument by which that would come about.

I look back with pleasure and satisfaction at the many times over a period of nearly twenty years in which I was in Mr. Wright's presence. Those hours were always special, and because of this I remember vividly the conversations, the amusing anecdotes, and the small talk, the easy banter between us. Although there was a great disparity in our ages and experiences, we were still able to work for mutual benefit: I to document his life and work, and he to leave me with an invaluable treasure of images and memories.

Even after all this time, I remember—almost feel—the initial excitement of having been part of a great experiment, a participant in a noble ideal, the Taliesin Fellowship. But even more than that, there is engraved in me, as deeply as it is carved in the massive lintel in the Hillside drafting room at Taliesin, the adage, "What a man does that he has."

On reflection today I can almost picture in my mind the scene of my embarking on my first trip to Taliesin West—wherever it was—and I know now what I did not know then: that I would be arriving at the Wright place, at the right time.

During all the years in which I contributed my photographs to the books of others, I longed for one of my own. That I have finally arrived at the end of this quest I owe to the encouragement and enthusiastic help of my very good friend Dixie Legler and also, in no lesser amount, to the vision and guidance of Diane Maddex. Without these two this book would have remained only a possibility stored away in the files and folders that I have described almost forever as "Yes, it's around here someplace."

Following Mr. Wright on his rounds in 1953 gave me the opportunity to photograph him supervising the wide variety of activities that went on at Taliesin: haying, the rebuilding of the theater, and, here, work in the drafting room at Hillside. His top draftsmen, John Howe to his left and Allen Davison on his right, watch as Mr. Wright checks over work he had previously assigned them.

11

INTRODUCTION

"Au revoir! Come back and see us!"

Frank Lloyd Wright stood on the concrete platform separating the desert from his civilization, Taliesin West. He faced west, toward the road I had just traveled, waving goodbye to departing guests. He wore a pair of loose-fitting khaki shorts, a white polo shirt, white ankle-length socks, and brown leather sandals. On his head was a tan porkpie hat. He leaned jauntily on a cane. In spite of his casual attire I was startled by his majestic presence.

His guests led a plume of dust as they headed west on the unpaved road. He watched them briefly and then turned his attention to me.

"And who are you?" he asked.

"My name is Pedro Guerrero," I answered. "I wrote for an appointment. I'm a photographer." I had never introduced myself that way before.

Without getting more than a fleeting glance at the spectacle that is Taliesin West, I found myself being led into Mr. Wright's studio. In spite of my newly acquired sophistication in art, I knew little about him. I set out my portfolio. While scanning it he made enthusiastic comments and questioned me about my origin and education. He was interested that I was a local and of Mexican descent—two truths that I did not, if I could help it, advertise.

"I see you have a fondness for the ladies."

My portfolio was a hodgepodge of school-inspired still lifes of commercial products, food, fashion, and an unnecessary number of nudes at a beach.

"Well, those were done in school—school assignments. I like women, of course, but I thought that the nudes show a proficiency that the ham and eggs don't."

"Are you married?"

"No, sir."

"How old are you?"

"Twenty-two."

"Well, don't marry until you're thirty and then marry a girl of nineteen. She'll keep you young. Young people today marry too early and then—right away—the babies. You're not in a hurry, are you?"

"No, sir."

While looking through my portfolio, Mr. Wright continued to chatter. He chortled at some of his own questions, my answers, and some secret raillery that our conversation inspired. I liked him instantly. He was unlike anyone I had known.

"What are you doing now?"

"Nothing. I'm unemployed."

"Would you like to work for us? We've just lost our photographer. He had some difficulty with women."

When Mr. Wright and I were at the Usonia site in Pleasantville, New York, in 1949, our photograph was taken by Keneji Domoto, an architect and former apprentice. Mr. Wright was on an inspection tour to see three of his houses taking shape. He congratulated me on the birth of my first child, a daughter. "You young guys," he joked, "get married and right away you start having babies." I protested: "Mr. Wright, this is my first child. By the time you had been married as long as I, you already had five." He just laughed.

13

What timing—what incredible luck!

"I'd love to work for you, but as you can see I have a lot to learn."

"I'll teach you. The pay isn't much, but you can eat here. You can start now."

It all happened so quickly. Within minutes of my arrival I had committed myself without hesitation to an offer of work so undefined as to be abstract. If the pay wasn't much, what was it exactly? What was this place? And for whom would I be working?

My arrival at Taliesin West in December 1939 was indeed a great stroke of luck. Just two years earlier Frank Lloyd Wright and his Taliesin Fellowship (his group of apprentices) had established a winter home in Arizona rather than spend the entire year at Taliesin, in Spring Green, Wisconsin. Mr. Wright had experienced the mild Arizona winters earlier, first in 1927, when he collaborated with Albert Chase McArthur on the design of the Arizona Biltmore in Phoenix, and again in 1929, when he was preparing drawings for the resort hotel San Marcos in the Desert, a project doomed by the stock market crash. A bout with pneumonia and the advice of doctors prompted him to return to Arizona to look for property on which to build. From 1937 until his death in 1959 Taliesin West was under construction, continually being changed by Mr. Wright. During this time he and the Fellowship spent half of every year in Arizona; during the other half they lived and worked at the original Taliesin.

With the recent completion of such acclaimed projects as Fallingwater in Mill Run, Pennsylvania, the Jacobs house in Madison, Wisconsin, and the Johnson Wax Administration Building in Racine, Wisconsin, Mr. Wright was regarded by many as America's greatest architect. This was a remarkable comeback for a man who had so recently been considered the "old man" of architecture. But here he was, at age seventy, embarking on a new

phase of his career and a new challenge—the construction of Taliesin West on eight hundred acres of rock-strewn desert in the foothills of the McDowell Range.

Taliesin West was only twenty-four miles from the place I called home for twenty years—Mesa, Arizona—a place I had fled in despair less than three years earlier. The second of six children, I was born in Casa Grande, Arizona, in a rude shack my father built for three hundred dollars. Soon after I was born my father, a foreman in a lumberyard, was transferred to Mesa. He traded the house and half a dozen chickens for a used Model T and moved the family the forty-mile distance. A few years later my father indulged a fancy that he was an artist by declaring himself a sign painter. A man of enormous charm and industry, he established a highly successful sign shop and by the 1930s became a respected member of the business community.

Although my siblings and I never lived in the barrio, we were still governed by all its constraints. We attended segregated schools, we were not permitted to swim in the municipal swimming pool, and we were to sit only on the left side of the movie theater, the section designated for Mexicans, blacks, and the occasional Pima Indian. But our family did not suffer from want, and we were among the handful of Mexican children who completed high school.

Graduation presented me with a problem: I had no idea what I would do next. College was never an option. My teachers did not suggest it. My father and mother, who had an eighth- and third-grade education, respectively, did not think of it, and neither did I. I accepted my diploma and spent the next two years of my life playing musical chairs with the few jobs available in that one-street town.

Career choices are the playthings of chance. I made a snap decision to pursue a career in art, not because I believed that I had any special talent but because it seemed exotic and I thought that the exotic was not bound by prejudice. So one day, without warning or discussion, I announced to my parents that I would be leaving Mesa to prepare for a career in art. I set my sights on the Art Center School in Los Angeles.

I left Mesa in 1937 on the night of my twentieth birthday. Two days later I arrived at the Art Center School unannounced and without the slightest idea of what I wanted to study under the broad category of art. I was informed that the art courses were filled.

"What else do you teach?"

"Well—photography."

"I'll take anything to keep from going back home."

Photography was foreshadowed by several incidents, one as early as first grade. By chance I discovered that when the door to the boys' toilet was shut, images from the outside—including my schoolmates at play—were projected onto the walls, ceiling, and floor through a tiny hole in the door. As if by magic the entire room was transformed into a camera obscura. I was mesmerized by this spectacle. Some years later, at the final awards assembly at Mesa High School, the art department awarded the outstanding art student a box camera. I was the recipient of that auspicious trophy.

From the Art Center School I called my father and told him that I was going to be a photographer—and to send a camera. My impulsive choice baffled him almost as much as my sudden departure from Mesa, but he obliged me. In photography I again found the enchantment I discovered so long ago staring at the images projected through a hole in the toilet door.

At school in Los Angeles there was enough to learn to consume four years of study: optics, emulsions, film speeds, chemical formulas, time and temperature ratios, light, shadows, lighting, logic, composition. But I was impatient. At the end of my second year I received a less than enthusiastic critique of my work and left the school in a fit of pique. So in the summer of 1939 I went back home to Mesa.

While waiting for something to happen, I built a darkroom behind our garage. I had no idea how I would find work. I thought about becoming a newspaper photographer, but after racing home to get a camera to photograph an overturned car I crossed off that idea. Father was understandably impatient with my indolence. He sensed even before I did that something drastic had to be done. As it happened, he had painted a sign years before, in 1928, to mark the site of Ocatilla, the small tent city that Frank Lloyd Wright and his draftsmen built while working out the details for San Marcos in the Desert. Father told me that Mr. Wright had a school somewhere in the valley beyond Scottsdale, and he wondered if perhaps there might be something there for me to do.

Father had often seen Mr. Wright at the Elquest Paint Company in Phoenix. The next time Father went to the store he asked Mr. Elquest for Mr. Wright's address. Mr. Elquest also gave him a letter of introduction, which I enclosed when I wrote to request an appointment.

"Yes," Mr. Wright wrote back. "Come any time."

So, on a morning of unimagined importance to me, following some general directions I set out to find Frank Lloyd Wright. In those days Scottsdale was an insignificant byway: a general store with a gasoline pump out front, three or four retail businesses, and an ice house. Houses were scattered about as if by an ill wind. As I drove along I came upon the occasional adobe ranch house squatting on the shaved desert floor. Otherwise the tawny, sere, caliche surface was broken only by brush— tumbleweed, paloverde, mesquite—and various forms of cacti. The unpaved but "improved" road ended a short distance north of Scottsdale. The McCormick Ranch was

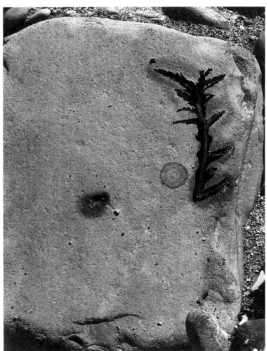

Had I known more about Mr. Wright when he interviewed me at Taliesin West in 1939, I certainly would not have shown him these samples from my portfolio of school assignments. That he hired me as an architectural photographer on the basis of these specimens testifies to the fact that he was an optimist.

TALIESIN WEST • PHOENIX ARIZONA

TO WHOM IT MAY CONCERN:

Pedro E. Guerrero was a student-apprentice (photography) in the Taliesin Fellowship under my direction for one year from May, 1940 to May, 1941. He left this work to join the army. While at work in the Fellowship he gave an excellent account of himself in every way.

Sincerely,
Frank Lloyd Wright
Frank Lloyd Wright, Architect
January 11th, 1942

Because I was going into the Army Air Corps from Taliesin, a letter of recommendation was hardly necessary. But Mr. Wright asked Eugene Masselink to type this letter for me. Mr. Wright made sure, however, that no one would mistake me for an architect—he personally inserted the word *photography*.

Ed Miller, a fellow student at the Art Center School in Los Angeles, took this photograph of me just as I finished setting up my camera on a class field trip to Malibu in 1939. I became an apprentice to Mr. Wright the following year.

the last outpost. At that point I turned right and followed a bumpy, twisting, rutted trail leading to the distant hills.

Eventually a perceptible horizontal slash in the foothills of the McDowell Range appeared. While weaving my way, I tried to imagine what I would find and I tried to practice what to say. Although I was a bit nervous about meeting Mr. Wright, I really knew very little about him. My first exposure to him had been through a traveling photographic exhibition at the Art Center School. The exhibit's architectural section included Hedrich-Blessing's famous image of Fallingwater, and in the portraiture section was a photograph of Mr. Wright himself. Both these photographs impressed me, but I did not connect the two until much later. Still, I was anxious about the impression I would make. The difficult terrain did not allow my mind to wander too much, however. At last I saw a reassuring sign, a symbol whose significance I was yet to learn. It was a patterned wood square measuring about two feet by two feet, painted red, mounted on a post and pointing to the nearby hills. After a few more minutes of wild, rock-strewn landscape I arrived at Taliesin West.

I found a parking space between two of a number of cars painted the same shade of red. Three people stood thirty feet away. I approached them with my portfolio of school photographs under my arm. That thirty feet was the final distance I would have to walk between a life of longing for change and an ever-expanding area of opportunity, challenge, and adventure.

My job interview with Mr. Wright lasted about fifteen minutes at most. Obviously, both of us were satisfied with each other.

"Start today," he said.

"I don't have my equipment. I'll be back tomorrow."

"Fine! I'll have Gene show you around. Gene," he called, "show this boy around the place."

He introduced us. "His name is Pete, and he'll be working for us."

Taliesin West opened up before me with Eugene Masselink, Mr. Wright's closest associate, as my guide. Gene wove me in and out of so much so fast that my first impression was surreal. Cortés could not have been more startled at finding the world of the Aztecs than I was in walking into an atmosphere that forever changed the way I looked on my own world. Nothing in my experience could have prepared me for this stunning complex of buildings. I realized that it was sculpture—a sculpture of canvas, redwood, and stone rising out of the desert. Taliesin West was molded from the desert too: its colors, its textures those of the ground from which it evolved. Its form echoed the surrounding gentle slopes and hills; it was as rugged and brutal as the rubble and spiny tangle on all sides. The swarms of young people who so lovingly labored there gave it scale, life, and boundary.

All around was a great confusion of activity. The dedicated bustle of so many young people was impressive, and I was apprehensive about how they would receive me. As we walked along I saw that forms were being built, cement was being poured, stones were being wheelbarrowed—all the functions of construction were being undertaken by the "boys," as Mr. Wright would forever refer to his apprentices. What I had first estimated to be hundreds were in fact only forty-five apprentices, mostly men, mostly indifferent to me.

Lunch did not dispel this impression. My introduction then did not lead to any friendly expression of welcome. It did not seem likely, in this sea of unresponsive faces, that there was one who might someday be a friend. The meal was not eaten in silence, but the language was strange and the jokes were incomprehensible. No one made the slightest effort to show me the minimal courtesy or acknowledge my presence. This was the Taliesin

Mr. Wright's studio and office at Taliesin West was bare and primitive, simply decorated with animal skins and desert plants. In 1947, when I documented the changes at Taliesin West over the past eight years, it was the same as the first time I saw it in 1939. In this room I met Mr. Wright and inflicted my portfolio on him.

21

Cane in hand—even in a canoe— Mr. Wright makes his way to a Fellowship picnic on the banks of the Wisconsin River near Taliesin. I shot this photograph in the summer of 1940 and was lucky to get it, given that I was out in the water myself.

Fellowship, and my reception was standard procedure. All outsiders—to the Fellowship, practically the whole world—were treated with icy aloofness until they were tried and found acceptable. It would be only a few short weeks before I, too, would react the same way to an even newer "fellow" than I.

I returned to Mesa late that afternoon. It was not possible to describe to my family exactly how I felt, what I had seen, and what it all had to do with me.

Once established as Mr. Wright's hired photographer and then as an apprentice in Arizona, I followed the Wrights and the Fellowship to Wisconsin in May 1940. There, as an official member of the Taliesin Fellowship, I spent the greatest part of my time in the photo lab, printing the images that I had photographed just weeks before in Arizona.

During this time my relationship with Mr. Wright was defined. After accompanying me to the Jacobs house in Madison. Wisconsin—my first assignment away from Taliesin—he finally decided that I could be trusted to photograph a house without his supervision. He wanted to include the Schwartz house in Two Rivers, Wisconsin, in an exhibition of his work to be held at the Museum of Modern Art, entitled Frank Lloyd Wright: American Architect (November 13, 1940, to January 5, 1941) and assigned me to photograph it. Later I photographed the Pauson house in Phoenix when we returned to Arizona that winter. For the most part I was left to my own devices. I had no budget (neither did he), but somehow he made it his business to keep me adequately stocked with film and other supplies. Mr. Wright simply mentioned what work he wanted done, and I decided how best to accomplish it.

In May 1941, after a prolonged personal struggle about whether to serve in the armed forces if the United States went to war, I left the Fellowship. In September I enlisted in the Army Air Corps. For fourteen months I was stationed at Lukefield Air Force Base in Phoenix, serving first as a photographic technician and then as a cadet. I was commissioned a second lieutenant at Yale University. In May 1942 the Air Corps assigned me to the Art Center School to do research in color printing, and there I met Barbara Haley Smith of Sterling, Colorado, a talented young painter. Between my tactical training at various posts here and my assignment as a photographic laboratory commander for a bombardment group in Italy, we were married. I was mustered out of the army as a captain in 1945.

Although marriage had ended any latent notion I might have had about rejoining the Fellowship, among my first acts on returning to civilian life was to pay my respects to the Wrights at Taliesin in Wisconsin. Mr. Wright, who had opposed the war, greeted me with the admonition, "Why didn't you go to jail like an honorable man?" Still, the visit went well, and Mr. Wright enthusiastically accepted my offer to be "on call" to him as long as he pleased. For the following fourteen years I continued my association with Mr. Wright, and he continued to occupy a place in my pantheon of heroes, a position he had to share with my father.

Immediately after the war I settled in New York City, where my wife had waited while I served in the army. Although the early quest for meaningful work was not easy, my portfolio of Mr. Wright's work opened doors wide if they opened at all. Once established as a freelance photographer in architecture, I completed assignments for most if not all the major architecture and shelter magazines—House and Garden, House and Home, Better Homes and Gardens, Architectural Forum, Architectural Record, Vogue, and Harper's Bazaar. My assignments also included photographing the work of other architects such as Marcel Breuer, Edward Durell Stone, and Philip Johnson.

As our family became too large to manage in a sixth-floor walkup apartment, my wife and I and our two children moved to the country. We bought and remodeled a small cottage on a low hill overlooking ten or so apple trees in New Canaan, Connecticut. We enlarged the house as our family grew by two more children. I commuted daily to New York, forty-five miles away.

Later I became enchanted with the work of two other important artists who also greatly influenced my life and my work: Alexander Calder, whom I met while on assignment for *House and Garden* and spent thirteen years photographing, and Louise Nevelson, whom I spent two years photographing. They, like Mr. Wright, were inventors of new art forms, and I found it exhilarating to be around such creativity.

All were equally passionate about their work but completely different in character. The elegant, almost foppish Mr. Wright was creative, resourceful, eloquent, and often imperious. The casual, earthy Calder, who gave wings to art as the inventor of the mobile, was also creative and resourceful but always unpretentious. Mr. Wright's tweeds, stiff collars, French-heel shoes, capes, cane, and rolled-brim porkpie hat were no more studied than Calder's flannel shirts (blue or bright red), chino pants, high-top brogans, and his thick shock of snow-white hair, but so comfortable was he with his image that I once saw a stack of brand new chino pants next to a stack of red flannel shirts, looking exactly as they must have in the store where he bought them. Nevelson, also a driven artist, proud and vain, similarly guarded her image—the absurdly long, gravity-defying lashes, her body wrapped in layer on layer of multicolored, multitextured fabrics, her head bound in a gray babushka. She too invented her art form, calling herself "the first recycler." Gracious and affectionate, she insisted on being called by her first name, just as Calder insisted on being called by his nickname, Sandy.

Frank Lloyd Wright, of course, was never just "Frank."

Decked out in a white summer suit and a gardenia boutonniere, Mr. Wright plays the organ at the 1940 wedding of apprentices Germaine Schneider and Rowen Maiden at Unity Chapel, near Taliesin. Always dapper of dress and demeanor, even in his most relaxed moments, Mr. Wright was a casting director's dream of what an architect should look like.

On one of my visits to Taliesin West I asked Mr. Wright in 1947 if he would allow me a few minutes to do a portrait in his studio.

"Oh, Pete, do you really think we need one?"

"Why not? Unless, of course, you feel you can't, or won't."

"Well, let me think about it. I'll call you."

"I'll remind you."

I went off to kill time, visiting old friends and busying myself shooting details with the small hand-held camera. Sometime after lunch I reloaded the camera and was hunched over some insignificant object about to be made into an insignificant picture when Gene Masselink called and said Mr. Wright was ready. "He doesn't think much of the idea, so do it quickly."

I saw by my exposure counter that I had two frames left. "Damn—I had hours to prepare for this!"

I grabbed two flash bulbs, hardly what I wanted to use, and went in. Mr. Wright was sharpening a pencil.

"What do you want me to do?" he asked, looking up. Flash.

"Exactly what you're doing," I said. Flash.

"Does that do it?"

"Yes, thank you."

He had removed his glasses and placed them on his desk. "I use them only to see with—not to be seen in," he said.

I returned to New York, and in a week or so I sent Mr. Wright the results. The first shot, had it been the only one, was good enough, but the second shot was superb! Later that year I saw him in New York. Commenting on the portraits he said, "You're little, but oh, my." And lucky, too, I thought—I might have failed completely if I had had more time.

TALIESIN WEST

When I made my second visit to Taliesin West in late 1939, it was to take my place as Mr. Wright's photographer. I was on my way not so much to a new life but away from an old one. Two years removed from the job of a shoe clerk in a dead-end town, I found myself with newly acquired skills and an opportunity of immeasurable potential. Taliesin West was as much a change and a challenge for me as anything in my life had been before.

The main structure—the drafting studio—was basically a glorified tent with roofs made of hinged wooden frames covered with canvas that could be opened or closed depending on the prevailing breezes or threat of rain. The canvas roofs leaked, of course. Because rains often followed desert storms, the canvas was stained with reddish swirls, giving the interiors a diffused light. The angular walls were made of the abundant red and gray desert stones—some of gigantic proportions—found on the site. These were placed in plywood forms filled with a mixture of desert sand and cement. When the forms were removed, the color and shape of the walls reflected the surrounding landscape.

The furnishings were designed by Mr. Wright and also built with apprentice labor. Long redwood benches were covered with boldly patterned ecru and burgundy fabric matching the colors of the shag rugs placed on the rough concrete floors. Calf and sheep skins were scattered throughout. Augmenting the benches were angular cushioned hassocks of redwood. Small redwood side tables held vases of desert flora, Chinese objects that had caught Mr. Wright's fancy, or colorful bowls of grapefruit and oranges.

The fact that Taliesin West was being built entirely by Mr. Wright's apprentices was in keeping with his philosophy of "making the whole man." Ironically very few of the apprentices involved in the intense labor of building Taliesin West were actually sheltered by it. Most lived in tents away from the main structure or were in the process of completing stone and canvas shelters of their own in the desert.

With very little time to prepare I threw myself into my new life and the huge assignment of photographing Taliesin West. The challenge seemed infinite; every facet of photography that I had been exposed to, as well as some new ones, was to be put into practice. One hurdle was Mr. Wright's insistence that I use an old 5-by-7-inch camera he owned and that, he alleged, "took good pictures." Later he released me from this curse when I threw one of his many homilies back at him: "It's not the pencil but the man."

Until then, however, I was compelled to use that unfamiliar, unwieldy camera with only one lens and that devoid of a shutter. I was forced to use a lens cap for all

At the beginning Mr. Wright did not really define what I was to photograph. "Do whatever moves you. Everything here is important," he told me. I realize now that he was just testing me to see what kind of an eye I had for taking photographs. I considered it important to document the construction going on around me and took a number of shots of the apprentices building Taliesin West. As the work continued over the years, I captured the additions and changes as well, such as this construction in progress in 1947.

29

my exposures. With film as slow as it was then, it took patience and skill to do anything other than long exposures. And yet I know that I did some of my finest work at that time.

I worked very hard. The desert sun was both a friend and an enemy. The contrast between light and shadow was extreme, and the film, mostly black and white, could barely cover the range of values in between.

Mr. Wright's promise to teach me what I needed to know did not come about in the traditional way. His only instructions were, "Photograph everything and anything that interests you. Show me what you can do." He did not tell me why he wanted me to photograph Taliesin West, but later I learned that this work, along with photographs of other projects, was for an exhibition at the Museum of Modern Art in New York City the following year.

My mistakes, of which there were a few, signaled my need for lessons.

"You must remember that I design everything sitting at a drawing table. I don't want bird's-eye—or worm's-eye—views of anything. When I want to see something from above we'll hire a plane."

"I must see one terminus. I prefer two, but one will do."

"We shouldn't have any trouble. Your eye level is close enough to mine." (This remark was his response to my wondering if I was too short to be an architectural photographer.)

"Don't think of yourself as short. Think of anyone taller than you as a weed. I do."

My work was unsupervised, so the photographs I periodically presented to Mr. Wright were my conceptions and my compositions. Now and then I would show up with one that would displease him. On one occasion he asked me to destroy a photograph I had worked very hard to create.

"It doesn't work. It is not of my architecture. It is not what I want you to tell me."

I put the photograph aside, but I did not destroy it. I liked it, even if Mr. Wright did not. I decided that I would bring it to him another time, and perhaps the second time around he would see the merit in the results of my fevered labors.

"Pete, I thought I told you to destroy this."

"You did, but I thought—"

"Well, now, you have got to stop thinking that just because you worked very hard on something that is reason enough to think it has some worth. We've gone over why it fails, so tomorrow you will bring the negative to me and we will destroy it together."

Mr. Wright was usually generous with his praise. He never rejected a photograph without explaining why. He had experimented with photography at one time and knew enough to be technically conversant, although not entirely in modern terms. He once showed me a few "bromides" of leaves and details of weeds he had photographed around his first home in Oak Park, Illinois. They were quite good, and he seemed very pleased that I told him so.

It was ironic that I should find myself so happily occupied studying shadows, patterns, and angles when so recently I had tortured myself with doubts of my ability. The absence of laboratory facilities at Taliesin West made it necessary for me to return each evening to Mesa, the scene of those doubts. Although I spent weekends there, all my time was devoted to processing the images I had taken at Taliesin West.

My routine made it difficult to develop friendships at Taliesin. After a month I still knew only Mr. Wright and Gene Masselink and very casually one or two others. What I could make of Fellowship life as I observed it from my distance gave me the impression that it was a discipline with many rewards. Everyone appeared to work very hard and participated in all aspects of what it took to make the organization function. And they all seemed to enjoy it. Some worked on construction, some in the drafting room, and some in the kitchen, and others seemed assigned exclusively to the rock pile.

Gene, more than any other apprentice, sacrificed his talents as a promising artist to serve as Mr. Wright's primary assistant and personal secretary. A charming, witty man, he was also a good baritone. William Wesley ("Wes") Peters, one of the first apprentices, was a brilliant engineer who was married to Svetlana, Mrs. Wright's daughter by a previous marriage. More than six feet tall, he towered over all of us, including Mr. Wright. Other apprentices at the time included John Lautner, John Howe, Edgar Tafel, Aaron Green, Alfred Bush, Ben Dombar, Kenn Lockhart, John de Koven Hill, Jim Charlton, Hulda and Blaine Drake, Cornelia Brierly, Marcus Weston, Fred Benedict, Burt Goodrich, Bob Mosher, Bob May, Anton and Honore Beck, Curtis Besinger, Gordon Chadwick, Herbert Fritz, Cary Caraway, and Allen and Kay Davison.

I became convinced that I had found what I was seeking, only a few miles from my home. I resolved to talk to Mr. Wright about my interest in becoming a member of the Fellowship.

Lunch, my only meal at Taliesin West, was still a lonely experience. Gradually, however, as I became more comfortable with Taliesin, Taliesin became more comfortable with me. As Mr. Wright continued to receive my batches of photographs with enthusiasm, the fellows began to accept me. Two months into my duty I was asked, at last, to join the group for the ritual of afternoon tea.

Tea was at four. It marked the end of the formal work day. The drafting room, the scaffolds, and the kitchen were abandoned for the lure of cookies, cake, and conversation. It was at tea that I was first introduced to Mrs. Wright, a woman of great poise and beauty. She was gracious and charming and asked about me—but carefully, not wishing to make me the center of attention. After tea the Fellowship dispersed to participate in whatever musical practice or rehearsal they were obligated to attend. With the day's accumulation of film to be processed I left for home.

After about three months, having at last become a familiar sight at Taliesin West and having managed to overcome some of my shyness, I began to lengthen my day. On several occasions I did not leave for home until well after dinner, to which I had not yet been invited. I discovered the beauty of Taliesin and the desert at dusk. I became fascinated with the possibilities—and difficulties—of photographing it in that rapidly changing light.

As I was taking pictures one Friday evening Mr. Wright came upon me.

"Well, the photografter is out late." (Mr. Wright delighted in calling me a photografter.) "That looks good." He approximated the camera's view through a frame he created with his hands.

"I hope it works. I've never tried taking photographs at this time of day before."

"These are the golden hours of the day," he said. He stood by me for a while, watching me closely. I took my photograph and prepared to move to another site.

"Pete, you should plan to spend the weekend with us sometime. It's a shame you have to drive home every night."

"I would enjoy that very much."

"Well, then, come tomorrow. Tell Gene to fix it up for you to stay with one of the boys."

Taliesin West was only half-completed at the time, and guest rooms as such were very limited. I knew from my wanderings that most of the boys had built some form of private shelter away from the main buildings. Some were quite elaborate, others little more than lean-tos in the process of becoming individual works of art. I did not feel that I knew any of the apprentices well enough to expect such a favor. So rather than have one of them placed in the awkward position of having to share his quarters with me, I decided not to spend the weekend and just told Gene that Mr. Wright had asked me to come for the Saturday night festivities.

A fire burned in the huge fireplace under the movie screen of the Kiva theater. I had often passed this windowless block house but had not explored its function; I had assumed that it was a storage room. That Saturday night I was introduced to its true purpose. Saturday was the day designated for such mundane activities as doing laundry, going into Phoenix for a haircut, or working on one's personal quarters—building on or shoveling out.

It was also a day for metamorphosis. Although I did not know everyone by name, I had become accustomed to their faces. That Saturday night, however, it required a second look to recognize any of them in their new guises. The half-clad, sweat-smeared laborers of yesterday had been transformed. Scrubbed clean, dressed in jackets, ties, and long pants instead of shorts, and chatting and laughing casually with the equally well-groomed women, they seemed to me again to be complete strangers. The fire in the great fireplace, spitting and crackling, added drama to their transformation.

When all the apprentices were in their places, Mr. and Mrs. Wright made their entrance; all stood in place as they entered. After a pause to admire the evening's decorations and reply to the murmured "Good evening," they proceeded to the highest level of the Kiva, where they sat in a specially decorated box of almost regal

splendor. From that height everyone was within their view; nothing escaped them. Dinner was served by the apprentices whose duty for the week was to prepare and serve the food.

Dinner offered an opportunity to introduce and welcome special guests. That night it was my turn. Mr. Wright introduced me as Pete.

"Frank, his name is Pedro," Mrs. Wright remonstrated. "Call him Pedro. Why do you call him by that cowboy name?"

She was to lose that battle. Mr. Wright called me Pete to the very end. (Because Mr. Wright seemed to me to run the Fellowship single-handedly, I gave little thought to Mrs. Wright. I had not yet cultivated friends who might have enlightened me about her importance, and I was too preoccupied with my own duties to realize that Mrs. Wright supervised most of the activities outside the design studio. This habit of unintentionally slighting her was something I would eventually regret.)

When dinner was over, the trappings and utensils of the meal were removed. A chorus of apprentices entertained us until all, including those on kitchen duty, were back in their places. The fire still burned beneath the movie screen but not with any intensity. The movie began.

A broad band of red fabric bordered the left side of the screen. Mr. Wright had asked someone to notch the projector so that the lines of the sound track would be visible, and these were projected on the fabric, running simultaneously with the images. Those ninety minutes were punctuated by enthusiastic quips or disapproving snorts from the master.

The movie ended. The evening was over. I headed back home, my head reeling from the evening's enchantment. I knew it had to be unique. It seemed incredible that it should be happening to me.

By the time I reached home that night I had decided

By 1959, when I
revisited Taliesin
West, movies were
33   shown in the Cabaret
■   theater rather than in
■   the old Kiva.
■
■
■

to ask Mr. Wright how I could become a member of the Fellowship. I had been hired as a photographer and had not discussed wages or terms, but suddenly those particulars seemed unimportant.

Part of the evening's conversation had dealt with the Fellowship's migration to its summer quarters—the other Taliesin in Wisconsin. That appeared to be something I should investigate as a means out of my personal desert. Mr. Wright continued to be enthusiastic about my work for him, so it seemed appropriate to broach the subject.

As the Fellowship's departure drew closer, I worked long and hard to prepare a new batch of photographs, a mixture of construction shots and architecture. I arranged to show them to Mr. Wright. He liked them. And then I asked him:

"How do I become a member of the Fellowship?"

In contrast to all his friendly informality up to that point, Mr. Wright was suddenly formal.

"We require two character references," he said, "and one letter of introduction—the fact that Mr. Elquest recommended you will do. Get two references, and then we will consider you."

I went home early that day rather crestfallen and asked my father for advice. He was unfazed. In a very short time he had helped me secure two letters—one from Robert Jones, the governor of Arizona, and one from Raymond Carlson, editor of the magazine *Arizona Highways* and a future Wright client. Armed with these, I returned to Taliesin West.

"Well, well," harrumphed Mr. Wright. "Is this the best you could do?"

"I think they're pretty good considering the short time."

"On our application [I had not seen one] we mention the sum of $1,100 tuition." Whatever hope I had vanished. "But we do have some apprentices who can't afford the tuition and work it off on a schedule. Can you afford it?"

"No."

"Well, in your case, since you are offering us your talents as a photographer, I guess we can waive the tuition."

"My God! Thank you! Now what do I do?"

"Start packing. We'll be leaving next week."

"You mean I'm accepted?"

"Of course."

There was no ceremony, no handshake—just a twinkle-eyed smile. And so I belonged. It appeared that, at least in my case, Mr. Wright alone could decide who was accepted and who was not.

A week later I moved my belongings onto an open balcony terrace that connected the Fellowship quarters with the family quarters. I rolled out my blankets to spend my last night in Arizona for a number of months. It was, in fact, my first and last night at Taliesin West.

All the typical fears of the unknown were the specters that kept me awake that night. Mesa was out there across the chill desert air and the waterless Salt River. In the morning, early, I would throw my bedroll, suitcase, cameras, hopes, and apprehensions into one of the cars of the caravan. I was off to greener pastures.

Alfred Bush, a New Yorker, was one of the many young apprentices who toiled mightily in the Arizona sun creating the Camp, as Taliesin West was then called. Here he fastens a rectangle of redwood scrap to the roof extension of the apprentices' dining room. Before it became known as Taliesin West, names such as Shangri-la and Aladdin had been suggested.

While compiling images in 1947 for a *House and Garden* special issue on Frank Lloyd Wright, I documented the building of a connecting bridge from the main Wright quarters to the senior apprentices' apartments. Here Wes Peters empties his wheelbarrow into the waiting forms.

An apprentice (above) paints one of the design elements used on the overhangs at Taliesin West. Lee Kawahara (left) waits for word to lift one of the stones at his feet into a predetermined position.

Taliesin West at the very beginning, as I saw it in 1940, was canvas, redwood, and stone. To catch the prevailing breezes, the canvas roofs and window coverings were designed to open and close by a series of ropes and pullies. The abundant desert flora was a fitting setting for this rugged structure. The pool (opposite) was a necessary extravagance on this arid and isolated site: it served as a source of water in the event of fire. A reflecting pool two feet deep, it was filled with water that had to be pumped from great depths.

38

This photograph
of the entrance to the
drafting room first
appeared in the 1940   40
MoMA exhibit of   ■
Mr. Wright's work.   ■
                             ■
                             ■
                             ■

As I became more comfortable with my surroundings, I began to realize what a marvelous opportunity this new job provided for testing my training. Here were interrupting forms, studies of texture and shadows, and the entire spectrum of values from black to white to test my techniques and the limitations of film and paper. The sun was directly overhead when I took this view of the bell tower—exploding the theory that photographers should put away their cameras at high noon.

Among the many new elements of design that caught my interest in 1940 were the playful pendants that hung on the buildings and swung in the wind. Made of wood, rope, and wire eyelets, they were meticulously painted in gold and muted colors. The buildings themselves certainly were not forms that described a dwelling to me. Shapes like those I found in the view from the drafting room looking past the dining room and to the uninhabited valley beyond (opposite) were both a challenge and an enchantment.

42

The living room
later was divided into
small seating areas,
and some of this   44
apprentice-built furni- ■
ture was replaced.   ■
                         ■
                         ■
                         ■

One side of the room
was designated as
the music area, domi-
nated always by the
master's piano and,
in 1940, a harp.

45

The drafting room in 1940 (opposite) reflected the fact that more work was being done outside to build Taliesin West than inside to complete commissioned projects. There was ample room for the twelve-foot-square model of Broadacre City, a grand piano, and a large presentation table. By 1947, which marked only the second stay in Arizona for the Wright entourage since the war, there still had been too little time to adopt organic refinements everywhere. Here in daughter Iovanna Wright's bedroom a single bare lightbulb with a string pull switch passes as lighting.

All apprentices were assigned weekly household tasks, including kitchen duty, an undesirable but necessary job. In addition to helping prepare food, the apprentices were expected to serve it. Each apprentice had to wash his or her own dishes, but everything else, including washing the pots and pans, was the responsibility of the day's kitchen help. The routine did not change much between 1940 (opposite) and 1947, when I revisited Taliesin West.

The caravan trips from Arizona to Wisconsin, having been made the three previous years, were efficiently executed. The lead car was Wes Peters's Cherokee-red Mercury. For part of the trip I was assigned to ride in a pickup truck and then in the station wagon near the back of the caravan, along with the Wrights' collie, Tweep, Mrs. Wright's parrot, Lulu, and apprentices Kenn Lockhart and Jim Charlton. It was Jim's misfortune to have the duty of caring for both Lulu and Tweep, who was reputed to be a poor traveler and needed daily doses of mineral oil. Jim also took it upon himself to teach Lulu to talk during the trip, fortunately without success.

Our route took us through northern Arizona and New Mexico's Indian country, to Dodge City, Kansas, and through Iowa's Amish country. We could take side trips from the caravan but were required to stop at the predetermined places where we would camp.

When the caravan stopped at night, the cars were parked encircling the makeshift kitchen a well-provisioned, specially designed mobile pantry mounted on the rear of a small pickup truck known as the Dinky Diner. The kitchen was the center of life on the trip. Doors opened down to serve as a work surface, revealing a gas stove, pots and pans, a coffee urn, and all other utensils and supplies sufficient to feed us supper and breakfast. Lunch was a fending-for-oneself affair.

At night we slept in bedrolls on the ground. The long evenings before sleep would overtake us afforded me an excellent opportunity to get to know my fellow travelers better. One by one they became aware that I was now a real part of their group. And no sooner was this fact discovered by the person in charge than I was put on the duty roster. But duty on the road was pretty much determined by the need to spell each other driving and to keep each other awake. Staying awake was easy for me—the caravan took us through landscapes I had not experienced before.

It did not look like much, but this was the Dinky Diner we depended on for meals on our trek east. On the third morning of our trip to Wisconsin, we stopped for breakfast in an open field near Dodge City, Kansas. In Indian country (opposite) some of the trucks were running too hot, so we stopped to put water in the radiators. From the left are John de Koven Hill, Bob May, Gene Masselink, Kenn Lockhart, and Jim Charlton.

TALIESIN

We arrived in Wisconsin in early May 1940. I had never seen a real spring before. Arizona's eternal sunshine and mild winters allowed for only the most subtle change of seasons. Here maples and oaks in feathery new leaf replaced saguaros, mesquites, and greasewood. Forsythia, quince, and dozens of other shrubs new to me were in flower. The mornings were cool—cold, really—but even cold was a new experience.

We drove over gentle hills, bisected occasionally by deep, dark ravines clad that May morning in forests of newly leafing hardwoods. From the crests of these hills we could see broad, flat valleys of earth so rich that it appeared black, neat farmhouses with huge red barns, and herds of cows grazing on grassy terraces. These were images I had seen before only on calendars. The small, clean, orderly towns, separated from the farmlands only by a buffer zone of farm equipment sales offices and the ubiquitous creameries, were a contrast to the service-station oases that dotted the inhospitable Arizona desert.

Taliesin was originally built by Mr. Wright in 1911 but was twice destroyed by fire—once in 1914 and again in 1925. A complete country estate, it included his home and studio, stables, garages, workshops, and other farm buildings as well as the Fellowship dining room.

We approached Taliesin by way of Hillside School, a group of structures that, I learned, was to be home. The buildings had been designed as the Hillside Home School by Mr. Wright in 1902 for his aunts, Nell and Jane Lloyd Jones. The school had recently been restored and enlarged to accommodate the needs of our group.

Hillside was only one of three clusters of buildings that made up our domain. Located at the western edge of the complex, it contained a theater, a huge drafting room, apprentice quarters, the photo laboratory, and a large number of rooms not yet assigned a function. Beyond Hillside was Midway, the farm complex that included a house for the tenant farmer and his family, barns, silos, and farm equipment sheds. Beyond Midway was Taliesin, Mr. and Mrs. Wright's quarters and the most important building in the complex. Taliesin, a Welsh word meaning "shining brow," nestled on the sunny crest of the highest hill. An exquisite house of golden sandstone and cypress, it overlooked the Wisconsin River to the north; its many decks and terraces provided a view of most of its nine hundred acres. This almost theatrical landscape afforded us a look at the changing seasons as we walked between Hillside and Taliesin many times daily.

Mr. and Mrs. Wright had traveled ahead of the rest of us, so when the caravan arrived in Wisconsin they were at Hillside to greet us. We were assigned to our quarters and were almost immediately organized by the duty roster. Taliesin came to life in amazingly short order.

Mr. Wright and some of his weekend guests enjoy the ritual of the Taliesin picnic in 1940. Unlike the daily picnic, which was planned for the convenience of the work crews, the weekend affairs took place in locations selected for their atmosphere. This picnic was held in the apple orchard; others combined lunch with a plunge in the Wisconsin River nearby.

55

There was work to be done in all directions—fields had to be plowed, crops planted, cows milked, and eggs gathered. In Arizona our preoccupation had been architecture and construction, but in Wisconsin farming—the production of food for our daily consumption and the canning of the surpluses that would sustain us in the desert—was our primary activity.

Life at Taliesin was as different from Taliesin West as their geography and architecture. There was more intimacy in the desert. Taliesin West was built in the manner of a fortress, all life radiating from it—but not too far. Unless one made a deliberate effort to hide, one seemed always to be under someone's watchful eye, which accounted for more friction and tension. Wisconsin's Taliesin, on the other hand, was a feudal country estate—of a benevolent master. And because we were spread out over such a vast area, we went about our tasks almost without supervision.

Bachelor apprentices lived in the resurrected remains of the Hillside Home School. Around the three sides of the great drafting room, which had been added in 1934, were our own private rooms. I was assigned to a gutted room containing only a mattress and a mirror. The outside wall was half window.

When an apprentice left the Fellowship for good, his quarters at Hillside were stripped down to the basics and assigned to a new fellow. We were expected to design and build these austere cells into something gracious and practical that would pass Mr. Wright's inspection. It didn't matter that I was a photographer with absolutely no training or ambition in architecture—that did not get me off the hook. Along with the others I was expected to work on my quarters in my free time. Mr. and Mrs. Wright would make frequent and unannounced visits to see how things were coming along.

The Wrights ate their breakfast and dinner separately from the Fellowship in a small room at Taliesin adjacent to the apprentices' dining room called, appropriately enough, the "little dining room." Occasionally they were served an entirely different menu from the Fellowship. Because Taliesin was intended to shape the complete human being, all of us were expected to be fully involved in every aspect of life there, not the least of which was serving the Wrights and their guests in the little dining room. This was to be our training in setting the table, arranging flowers, pouring wine, and serving.

At Hillside, the headquarters for all design activity, there was always at least a skeleton crew of apprentices busy drafting or delineating Mr. Wright's rough designs or working out the details of designs already approved. During the day the population here fluctuated depending on the urgency of Mr. Wright's commissions. But in the evenings, after dinner, the drafting room came to life; every one of the twenty tables was filled with apprentices working on projects, some finishing work left by other apprentices who had been called away from Taliesin.

Some apprentices almost always lived away from Taliesin, supervising buildings under construction. Wes Peters, for example, was working on the Pew house in Madison, and Edgar Tafel was supervising the Schwartz house in Two Rivers. It was Mr. Wright's policy always to have one of his "boys" directly in charge of each of his buildings. This was, needless to say, an important learning experience.

Construction always seemed to be going on somewhere at Taliesin during the summer of 1940. The married apprentice quarters, a long-abandoned dormitory designed by Mr. Wright in 1887, were in such a state of disrepair that they needed a major push just to make them livable. The apprentices were thrown into the breach as plumbers, electricians, plasterers, masons, and carpenters.

The lush, green landscape at Taliesin was originally as foreign to me as Taliesin West had been. But this Taliesin was a refined, serene place compared to the rough, exuberant Taliesin West. Farm work—with haying probably the most onerous—was an all-out activity for the Fellowship, one of the tasks necessary for a self-sufficient community. Here in 1953 Mr. Wright watches while rolls of hay are stacked.

After a Saturday picnic in 1953 Mr. and Mrs. Wright descend the steps from the tea circle to the main house, passing below the bell that summoned all to meals and tea and that signaled the official end of the work day. On this early fall afternoon Mr. Wright had removed his coat—but not his cap.

58

And there was always the possibility of an unscheduled emergency arising from an idea that might occur to Mr. Wright on one of his frequent walks through the buildings. This could involve anything from rearranging the playhouse's seating scheme to building a tower at Midway as a tribute to the cows in gratitude for a good year. Whatever occurred to his ever-active mind became an immediate priority.

One afternoon an apprentice asked me to assist in repairing a cantilevered table in Mr. Wright's study that had become unmoored from the wall. I was to hold the table in place from underneath while the other fellow attempted to screw it to a supporting stud. The screws turned out to be the wrong size, and I was instructed to stay put under the table, not moving a muscle, until he returned with the longer screws. Thus hidden from view, I was able to observe Mr. Wright when he entered the room a moment later.

He walked in briskly, dressed for the day in a starched collar, flowing tie, and tweed suit. His keen and critical eyes, ever alert to the slightest imperfection, fell on some objets d'art on a shelf. He glided to them and shifted them, one forward, one to the right. He walked backward, looking at them with his head tilted slightly, hesitated, and scooted toward them again but, deciding he was satisfied, glided to the piano and ran through a few bars of Bach. He cleared his throat, picked up his hat and cane, and disappeared out the door—in character all the way. He had played the classic Frank Lloyd Wright role as if he were before an audience, but I am certain that he thought he was alone.

Every afternoon, after most of the day's work was done, tea was served in the tea circle. This circle was situated under a huge oak on the crest of Taliesin's hill. From this spot, even when sitting on the ground, I could look over the roof of the family quarters and down on the panorama of green fields and wooded hills that extended for miles.

Mrs. Wright was always at tea, but not so Mr. Wright. I think he napped then. Mrs. Wright would preside and introduce us individually to guests. If one of us was from outside the United States, she would mention that also. She invariably introduced me as being from Mexico, which I did not bother to correct although it was not true by about four generations. She insisted on calling me Pedro, which I must admit was a bit grating to me. I was not yet so far removed from southwestern bigotry that I could accept without embarrassment attention being called to my Mexican name and my ethnic distinctiveness.

Here in the tea circle I became further exposed to the good life. The gardens, annuals planted in neat borders of carefully selected colors and great masses of volunteer bloom, grew as if Mr. Wright had told them where, how many, and how tall. And vines—vines were everywhere. Mr. Wright could not stand the look of a bare building. (Many vines that appear in photographs of his buildings, obviously too new for such foliage to have grown, were penciled in by him. A botanist would be hard pressed to identify them.) We discussed many things at tea. As the only unrushed time of the day that we were all together, it would have been a logical time for a pep talk or for chiding one of us for something. But such was never the case. Tea was always a time for anecdotes and laughter. An apprentice would recount an experience in dealing with a client or a local merchant, or Mrs. Wright would relate Mr. Wright's latest witticism. If we had a special guest, we would listen to and question him or her. And we often did have special guests: Sinclair Lewis, Lawrence Tibbett, and Charles Laughton, among others, visited while I was there.

It was in the tea circle that I finally felt I was a member in good standing of the human race. I was as much at ease with these people, who not long ago had been strangers, as I might have been among those with whom I had grown up—in fact, much more so. Here I was accepted completely for myself, for what I was. At the daily ritual of the tea circle I became aware of this acceptance.

Throughout the summer our ranks swelled with college students, relatives of the Wrights, and friends of the Fellowship who would join us for a week or two. For some reason the usual coldness to outsiders did not seem to apply to these transients, who gave us a renewed sense of fun. But with them that summer of 1940 came disconcerting news from the outside world that was subconsciously annoying although we outwardly discounted it: our country was mobilizing for war. It was inconceivable to me that Europe's problems had anything to do with us. Certainly worrying about them did not get the tomatoes picked or drawings completed. With the harvest approaching, the work in the fields was equal to that in the drafting room.

Most of the field work—in fact, practically all of it—went on without me. I was busy working in the nearly completed photographic laboratory, located in a seldom-visited section of Hillside. The nature of my work required that I spend many lonely hours of many lovely days shut up in a dark, airless room. Unless I was taking pictures, I had to stay indoors. I envied the others, who worked together in the great outdoors.

When I finally got outside, I plunged into the work, determined to harden up physically and get back some of my color. Architectural commissions were coming in so briskly that drafting was consuming the time of more and more apprentices. Wes Peters, who was in charge of all labor, was delighted to have me as a field hand and assigned me to the bulldozer. My duty was to destroy the fence lines that marked the boundaries of the property at the foot of the hill, which Mr. Wright had just acquired.

Trees averaging one foot in diameter had to be felled, and then their stumps had to be bulldozed out. In this job I was still alone, but at least I was outside and could hear the sounds of others at work.

Summer was waning. Until we were needed for final harvest we would have time for late afternoon rides around the Wisconsin countryside, a swim in the river, or, because the days were still long, a touch football game after supper. On Saturdays, when we were relieved of our regular duties, we might indulge in all these activities.

At this time and through the 1940s Taliesin had only one phone, a pay phone outside Mr. Wright's office. Given the complex of buildings and the number of people scattered over that many acres, it seems incredible that a single pay phone was the only voice connection we had with the outside world. But Mr. Wright abhorred being metered or getting routine monthly bills. He preferred to scrounge around for loose change when he needed to call someone. More than once I was solicited and temporarily relieved of the meager number of coins I had on me. Mr. Wright never failed to pay me back. How he kept track of ten cents here or twenty-five cents there seemed to be part of his genius.

The days continued to be fraught with anxiety about world events. In late August 1940 I fell into step with the dominating belief at Taliesin that if war did come we would resist the draft. We greeted with enthusiasm any plan that opposed the draft and then the war. We applauded discredited heroes such as Charles Lindbergh and supported his pleas that we stay out of Europe's war. At tea Mr. Wright would respond to our anxious questions:

"Oh, the draft won't pass!"

It did.

"Just don't register for it!"

A group of middle-aged men came to Hillside one day, and one by one we were registered.

"It is one thing to register, quite another thing to go. When you are called, then resist!"

Any dreams I may have nurtured about independence of thought or action as an adult were shattered, because my father persuaded me that I had an obligation to a group comprising about one-fourth the population of Arizona. He believed that Mexican Americans would be seen as unpatriotic if we demonstrated any resistance to the draft. The notion that the action of just one man would affect the lives of so many because of a common ethnic tie was not to be tested by me.

Mr. Wright made it clear that although he could not tell us what to do when the time came for each one of us, he could and would advise us that our only honorable option was to refuse to comply.

"Go to jail if you have to. You will always be welcome here."

That was no comfort to me. Mr. Wright's patriotism was old-fashioned. He believed that war had no place in a nation of intelligent, humane, and honorable people.

The summer ended, but our concern did not. We fell behind schedule, and it was some time after Thanksgiving before we left for Arizona. Mr. Wright had been absent a great deal during the summer and early fall tending to projects. A blizzard with waist-deep snow and subzero temperatures forced the move.

As was the usual practice we packed the trucks headed to Arizona with the bounty of the autumn harvest: canned goods, smoked meats, and homemade jellies. Among the items destined for consumption at Taliesin West in the winter were two five-gallon containers of honey. Near the end of the Fellowship's trip west, the honey was confiscated at the border by the Arizona agriculture department.

Mr. Wright summoned me to his office and rather testily told me to get hold of my "friend" the governor and tell him he had to release the honey at once. The governor, at my father's request, had written a letter of reference recommending me to Mr. Wright as a possible apprentice. But asking me to contact the governor was a tall order. How could I call the governor of the state of Arizona, who probably had more pressing matters to deal with than Mr. Wright's honey? I decided to do nothing.

As luck would have it, the agriculture department tested the honey, found it to be uncontaminated, and returned it a day or so later in an official Arizona agriculture department truck. Mr. Wright called me in again and thanked me. "It was nothing at all," I replied. "I was happy to do it."

Because I had not established a place to live at Taliesin West, I continued to reside at my parents' home in Mesa. I commuted there, as before, to photograph the Fellowship's activities and the continual changes to the property. As spring and the anniversary of my joining the Fellowship approached, I knew I would have to decide what my next move would be. The Fellowship would be going back to Wisconsin in May, and it seemed appropriate—if painful—for me to resign. I was certain I would be drafted. One day I took a pick and shovel with two of my closest friends at the Fellowship who, like me, faced a call to arms, and we busied ourselves digging a trench for a water pipe on a small rise out of sight of Taliesin. We took turns with the tools so that the sound of steel hitting stone could be heard continuously. It was hot work but required no concentration, and we three friends were able to discuss our dilemma. To ever again become totally immersed in the isolated work of the Fellowship without world events overtaking us seemed impossible. We decided to leave Taliesin at the earliest opportunity.

We agreed to tell Mr. Wright as soon as possible but no one else. As I asked Gene to arrange a few minutes with him, Mr. Wright overheard me and called me in. I talked with him about my long struggle with this issue. I told him how much I respected him and how much my year with the Fellowship had meant to me. After very painful soul searching I had decided to leave, but he had to believe that I was doing so with the utmost reluctance.

We talked for a long time. He told me that I should always consider myself a fellow in good standing and that I was welcome to return to Taliesin when and if I wished. He regretted that I did not see my way clear to resist the draft, but he knew that it was easier for him to say so than for me to do so; after all I had to answer to the charges that would be made against me.

We talked about my work. He said he was "pleased beyond all expectations." He added that I was a "fine boy" and that he would always be interested in what happened to me. We shook hands and said our good-byes. Then reaching into his pocket he took out two one-hundred-dollar bills, handed them to me, and said, "Take care of yourself."

I left Taliesin West without saying goodbye to anyone else. I left the way I had come, quietly and alone. But I was leaving better prepared for whatever lay ahead. I knew that once my military service was over I could return to Taliesin, go back to school, or, most alluring, seriously consider a career as an architectural photographer. Mr. Wright had been a good critic and teacher, objective about my efforts when we were on location.

As I drove away I could see that the trucks were being readied for the journey back to Wisconsin. The Fellowship would go soon. And war would break out before it was time for the Fellowship to return. Four years would pass before they would come back to Arizona. My life too would be disrupted for at least that long.

In his private study and bedroom at Taliesin, Mr. Wright—architect, collector, and farmer—prepares to begin his morning work surrounded by two of his many Japanese prints, an oarlock from a Venetian gondola, a collection of T-squares, and some ears of homegrown corn.

After being cooped up in the darkroom for many weeks, it was a relief to be outdoors running the bulldozer. The two weeks devoted to this field duty were as enjoyable as any I spent at Taliesin. There was pioneer satisfaction in opening new land and simplifying the vista from the Taliesin living room. Out of the photo laboratory and sitting astride a machine I could command, I felt all-powerful.

Unfortunately Mr. Wright directed one of his daily walks toward my project. I stopped the bulldozer and jumped off to greet him. He was startled to see me involved in this type of work, and although he approved of what I had accomplished he gave me to understand that I was about to separated from my new-found love. There were photographs to be taken.

We came upon a view of Taliesin with a small herd of cows in the foreground, and Mr. Wright instructed me to get my camera. "See how much more this view of Taliesin means with those cows in the foreground—see how they relate." Later I read his ode to cows in the section "To Her" in his autobiography. Here he described how a cow enhances a landscape:

"Why is any cow, red, black, or white, always in just the right place for a picture in any landscape? Like a cypress tree in Italy, she is never wrongly placed. Her outlines quiet down so well whatever contours surround her. A group of her in the landscape is enchantment."

As Mr. Wright and I continued to walk along the fence row, we talked about the land and the Fellowship experience and how I was progressing. Then we turned back. On the way he pointed out one view to be photographed and then another, all seemingly impossible compositions. He would wave his cane toward a broad vista, and I knew what I would be doing next.

I knew also that Mr. Wright would wave his cane toward the work the new bulldozer operator would be attempting, and it too would be done.

The many stone, cast-iron, and wood icons of Mr. Wright's vast collection of oriental art were scattered throughout Taliesin. Some stood on ledges, while others adorned specially constructed stone pedestals built into the walls. A cast-iron Buddha stood outside the entrance to the Taliesin residence (opposite). A large Chinese ceramic pot graced the top of the entry stairs (left), and one of Mr. Wright's many expensive automobiles was parked in the drive below. I took this photograph in 1947 standing on the top of the stairs, looking out toward the terrace of Mr. Wright's studio and the hills bordering the Wisconsin River.

Mr. Wright was obsessed with owning all the land that he could see from his living room window, the highest point at Taliesin. From his study and bedroom (opposite), a view taken in 1952, one can see the lake below and the hills beyond, all part of Mr. Wright's ancestral land. The stone that went to build Taliesin was quarried from land nearby. To contrast with its rough texture, Mr. Wright added delicate oriental sculptures and arrangements of flowers and natural elements.

Late in November 1940 I experienced my first snowfall. It snowed all night, and when I woke up the next morning the entire countryside was blanketed in white. I was so excited I just threw on my coat over my pajamas, grabbed my camera, and began taking pictures. I had never experienced such cold. When I was finally dragged back inside, my eyebrows were white and my breath had frozen to my muffler.

Even though I had been at Taliesin for seven months, it had not occurred to me to photograph Mr. Wright other than at picnics. The photograph of Mr. and Mrs. Wright in front of the Romeo and Juliet windmill is the first I took of either of them. I came across them walking with their dog, Tweep, while I was exuberantly photographing my first snow.

The Romeo and Juliet windmill was one of Mr. Wright's earliest architectural commissions. He designed it in 1897 for his aunts, Jane and Nell Lloyd Jones, who ran the Hillside Home School. A bold departure from the traditional steel-frame examples, the windmill was built completely of wood. The Lloyd Jones uncles, unlike the aunts, had little appreciation for or confidence in the design and predicted that it would fall during the next summer gale. It had already withstood the gales of forty-three summers when I photographed it in 1940.

Romeo and Juliet played an important role in our lives at Taliesin. Mr. Wright thought that the field workers should not be denied the pleasure of hearing the Bach and Beethoven records that were played continuously in the drafting room. His solution was to install a speaker, connected to the Scott record player in the drafting room, atop the Romeo and Juliet windmill, sited on Taliesin's highest point. The equipment was excellent, the records were superb, and the Wisconsin countryside came alive with music. Everyone was pleased—everyone, that is, except Mr. Wright's sister Jane Porter, whose house was immediately below and behind the windmill, and she objected in no uncertain terms to the loudness of the music. It amused us to see the indomitable Frank Lloyd Wright called to task by his angry, diminutive sister, but he took it good-naturedly.

Eventually she won out, but not until we had had full exposure to the complete works of Bach and Beethoven. Only then did Mr. Wright order the music stopped. But the summer was almost over anyway.

In the summer of 1940 the main activity of the Fellowship was model making for the MoMA show to be held later that year. Hans Koch, Marcus Weston, and Blaine Drake (opposite) work on the model of the San Francisco Call Building (1912), one of Mr. Wright's favorites (but never built). After the MoMA show the model moved between Hillside and his private studio at Taliesin, where it was displayed when I photographed the room in 1947 as I waited for Mr. Wright to consent to pose for a portrait.

75

Overlooking the Romeo and Juliet windmill a quarter mile away, this large room (opposite) was Mr. Wright's study, his private domain. Here his desk holds not just his writing instruments but the tools of his trade: triangles and T- squares. Beyond his desk was his daybed, where he, an early riser, needed time to regenerate after lunch.

Sunday night dinner in the great living room at Taliesin was the reward for our week's labor. The meal was the best culinary effort by the cook of the week. Bathed, shaved, and dressed in jackets and ties, we all gathered in the living room. There was a sense of anticipation as we stood around in our unusual finery awaiting the Wrights and their guests.

The evening would begin with a violin or piano solo by one of the apprentices or selections by a string ensemble composed of Fellowship members. Then the meal would be served on little tables while Mr. Wright and the guest of the week — and any apprentice who dared to join in — would entertain us with interesting and compelling conversation.

The moments before most of the apprentices arrived were, to me, the best part of the evening. Mr. Wright always arrived early, more often than not carrying a cup of coffee laced with brandy. He would straighten, tidy, and admire all the things he loved so much and stand at the window of this aerie looking down on the unending landscape of fertile Wisconsin land.

For many years this land belonged to his family. But now certain portions, not well kept, were no longer under family control. Some time later Mr. Wright purchased the farm at the very bottom of the hill just to tear down the eyesore of a house that stood there. The view was immensely improved, and he could look out the window and gaze only at land that was his.

One special Sunday night, when Ben Masselink, Jim Charlton, and I were serving, the food was so outstanding that it ran out completely. Mrs. Wright, coming in to congratulate the kitchen help, was dismayed to discover that there was nothing left for us to eat. "Ah," she said, "but you still have all this wine." Three pitchers and three of us. In due time we took off our aprons, put on our jackets, and staggered into the living room. Mr. Wright had us ushered out immediately.

In late September 1952 Mr. Wright asked me to photograph the Neils house in Minneapolis, but typically he insisted that I stop over at Taliesin and do some other work for him. I rephotographed many things during the visit, although the loggia, a sitting room with a balcony overlooking the pond, was a new subject for me.

Mr. Wright had a passion for exotic, expensive automobiles, but he also became intrigued with the Crosley, an inexpensive miniature American car. He ordered a number to distribute among the senior apprentices, keeping one for himself and Mrs. Wright. He also loved to ride horses. With the aid of apprentice Joe Fabris, groom for the summer and fall of 1953, and a mound of freshly graded earth, he mounted his favorite horse, Fleet (opposite). "How's this for eighty-six?" he later asked.

Our return to Arizona in the fall of 1940 was delayed, and we spent Halloween in Wisconsin. All design activity ended. With the farm also dormant a costume party of no specific theme was planned. Mr. and Mrs. Wright appeared in quasi-royal Montenegrin outfits (Mr. Wright adding to his height by wearing one-and-a-half-inch Cuban heels). I came as a sultan, and Jim Charlton was my dancing girl for the evening.

For a week we all worked feverishly decorating the living room and broad hallways of Hillside with pine boughs and huge oak branches and making our costumes. There was much wine and cider at the party. Kenn Lockhart, Kay Davison, and John de Koven Hill enjoyed it thoroughly. (They remain resident members of the Fellowship.) The evening's highlight was a production of *Our Town* in the Hillside playhouse by the Taliesin Players.

In the summer our kitchen abounded with fresh vegetables, and at times it was Mr. and Mrs. Wright's happy boast to a visitor that the meal just eaten had been entirely Taliesin grown. Except for the sugar and coffee, which we bartered for in Spring Green with our surpluses, everything was home grown. Even the wines were fermented in the large root cellar at Taliesin. Choices were made as to what to butcher—a calf, a pig, chickens.

The food, served in abundance, was prepared from the collection of Taliesin recipes that had been carefully worked out to serve our large number. At the height of the summer, when all the crops ripened, some dishes were prepared with so much care that the preparation itself became a ritual. When corn, for example, was to appear on the menu, the kitchen crew was dispatched to the fields in a truck to pick enough for the meal. The timing was such that huge pots of water would be boiling and ready to receive the ears, which the kitchen crew shucked on the way from the field. This process took about ten minutes. Meanwhile the rest of the dinner was cooked and ready to be served. The same ritual would apply to tomatoes, cucumbers, cantaloupe—all were picked vine-ripe and served minutes before the rest of the meal.

Lunch, as a convenience to everyone but those working in the kitchen, was held picnic fashion somewhere near the greatest concentration of activity—on the side of a hill near Hillside, on Midway Hill, near Taliesin, or at some site within walking distance of all three. Meals were prepared in the usual manner and transported to the preselected site in one of the Fellowship's many vehicles. During the week the paid workmen at Taliesin—masons, carpenters, and handymen needed to assist in the Fellowship labors—were invited to join in the picnic lunches. Only on weekends did we have the time to venture beyond our own grounds. We might go to the banks of the nearby Wisconsin River or to Borglum's Rock, a lovely wooded terrace some miles away on a sheer escarpment overlooking a breathtaking ravine.

The daily picnics were expertly organized. Once the food arrived at the site, everyone got into the spirit of things. It was a relaxing informal break that was always welcome. When the apprentices did not eat outdoors, they gathered in the apprentices' dining room, located in the tower apartments (opposite) for senior and married apprentices at Taliesin. Directly behind the statue is the entrance to the "little dining room," where the Wrights were served their meals—separately from the apprentices.

On a cool summer evening at Taliesin in 1948, Mr. Wright shares a number of his Japanese prints with his apprentices and reads to them some words of wisdom on the subject. At one time he owned one of the world's most distinguished collections of Japanese prints. Mr. Wright always tried to instill an awareness of the beauty and creativity to be found in every aspect of daily existence.

Earlier that afternoon in the Hillside drafting room, Mr. Wright reviews some drawings by apprentice Allen Davison based on Mr. Wright's own sketches. The child by his side is Davison's son, Tal. Mr. Wright thought of working and teaching as one and the same, so Taliesin life was built on the age-old master-and-apprentice relationship, which meant learning by doing, listening, and seeing.

From blueprints to models to full-scale construction, some type of building was always in progress at Taliesin. Apprentice John de Koven Hill (opposite) labors over a model in 1940. It was the Jester house, destined for the MoMA show. Mr. Wright himself found work in 1953 supervising the reconstruction of the Hillside playhouse, which had burned— a fate suffered by many structures at Taliesin. When I saw him here I really wanted to say, "Would you please take off that damned crocheted cap and go get a hat?" But I did not have the nerve.

BROADER ACRES

After I left the army in 1945 I picked up just about where I had left off: photographing Mr. Wright's buildings—now, however, well beyond the walls of the two Taliesins. Because he trusted my working methods and my ability to interpret his architecture, he always chose me whenever he had control over the selection of a photographer for a magazine article on his work. Sometimes he arranged to have the client or the magazine pay me. When I worked exclusively for him, we negotiated the fee. I told him that I would be satisfied if he just paid my expenses, and he reminded me that he fed and housed me and that I should deduct that from my fee. His method of payment had changed: earlier he usually handed me cash; now he paid by check.

My work on the road for Mr. Wright actually began in the summer of 1940, when I became the first to photograph in detail the first Jacobs house and the Pew house (then still under construction), both in nearby Madison. Mr. Wright also asked me to document the Schwartz house in Two Rivers, Wisconsin, for his 1940 exhibit at the Museum of Modern Art and to make progress shots of the Manson house, also under construction in Wausau, not far away.

Once I had received instructions for the Schwartz house, I gathered my equipment, and Mr. Wright and I went to the bank in Spring Green to get money for my trip. He handed me a one-hundred-dollar bill. That added to what cash I already had came to probably $102.45. Mr. Wright arranged for me to drive Wes Peters's brand-new Mercury convertible, which was painted a gleaming Cherokee red, Mr. Wright's favorite color.

I was twenty-three years old, short and swarthy, dressed in a crew-neck sweater, Levi's, and a pair of brown, unpolished oxfords. I did not look of Wisconsin at all. But that did not bother me in the least, because at the moment I was rich beyond belief, and I was loath to spend any of the cash in my pocket.

I had managed to arrive at the Schwartz house without spending a dime, but before I could leave for my next assignment I had to refuel. It was almost dusk, and as I was unfamiliar with the road I was anxious to be on my way. I drove into a service station and asked the attendant to "fill 'er up." I also asked him to help locate the light switch in the car. He obliged but asked, "Isn't this your car?" "Yes," I answered, "but it's so new I haven't driven it at night yet." At the time gas cost only about twenty-five cents a gallon, and my purchase came to about three dollars. I reluctantly handed him the one-hundred-dollar bill.

I was sure he had not seen too many one-hundred-dollar bills. To make change he had to go to several places around the neighborhood. I guessed that he might be

Mr. Wright's last twenty years were filled with innovative work in far-flung places. Among them were his Usonian houses, including the Usonia enclave in Pleasantville, New York, begun in 1947. Three houses, mostly of stone, were built there for the Friedmans, the Serlins, and the Reisleys. In 1952 he and his builder, David Henken (left) revised some of the Reisley house plans while Roland Reisley (center) watched. Mr. Wright added two feet to the chimney— a change that Henken thought unnecessary.

getting tired of me—and then I gave him even more reason to be suspicious. Mr. Wright had asked me to be home early on Saturday, the next day, and I figured I could make better time taking the back roads to Wausau. I asked the attendant for directions, which he gave with great enthusiasm—he was eager to get rid of me.

At the Wausau city limits I was greeted by a highway patrolman, who immediately placed me under arrest "for speeding," he said. "Whatever happened to tickets?" I asked indignantly. I followed him to the local jail.

From the type of questions I was asked I deduced that I was being held on suspicion of grand larceny—auto. Recalling my dumb behavior earlier that evening at the service station, I was sure of it. When asked whose car I was driving, I unaccountably answered, "Frank Lloyd Wright's." They did not book me because they were not sure what they could charge me with, and anyway there was no magistrate on duty at that hour of the night. So I was put into an unlocked cell. I could wander in and out and did so occasionally to ask what they had planned for me. No one asked what the likes of me was doing in Wausau, and it never entered my head to tell them. I sat in jail all night—"on suspicion."

After many changes of the guard someone came on duty who asked me what I was doing in Wausau. I told him I was there to photograph a house under construction. Whose house? I told him. As luck would have it, Mr. Manson was among other things a police commissioner. "Why didn't you say so?" asked my interrogator. "You could have saved us all a lot of trouble and probably, now, a lot of embarrassment." So it was Commissioner Manson, then? Well, no one had told me, and no one had asked me.

No one thought it appropriate to disturb Commissioner Manson at that hour, so I had to wait until morning anyway, when I was released to his custody. He thought the whole incident very amusing but warned, "You have embarrassed a lot of law officers, and they are going to be watching out for you." He evidently called Mr. Wright and told him everything—I certainly was not going to. Mr. Wright brought it up later, and it was obvious that he was not amused. I tried to explain, but he cut me off: "All you kids drive too damned fast." He was a good one to talk.

The photographs of the Schwartz, Jacobs, and Pew houses, as well as the photographs I had taken earlier in Arizona, had to be enlarged to 20 by 30 inches and mounted on plywood panels for inclusion in the Museum of Modern Art exhibit. The effort to photograph and then enlarge and mount so many images by myself consumed almost the entire summer. As a result I had little time to take other photographs. The show was finally assembled and trucked to New York City.

The last house I photographed before I left Taliesin to join the Army Air Corps was the Pauson house, which I shot in the winter of 1940–41. Although I visited both Taliesins in the interim, I did no more work for Mr. Wright until 1947, when some of his major buildings at Florida Southern College were at last completed.

House and Garden in 1947 asked me to meet with Mr. Wright to discuss a proposed issue devoted to his architecture. The plan did not succeed because there were not enough new or completed Wright houses in that postwar period to fill a whole issue. In preparation for it I did, however, photograph the Sturges house in Brentwood Heights and Arch Oboler's studio in Malibu, California.

Still hoping to make the issue a reality, I suggested to Mr. Wright that perhaps he could recommend some former apprentices whose work might appear with his to complete the issue. I should have known better. "No!" he answered emphatically. When I asked why, he replied, "Why should I put in a good word for the competition?"

This shot of the Manson house did not merit my spending a night in jail, but it was a learning experience anyway.

Arch Oboler, a Hollywood writer and producer of mostly science fiction films, commissioned several designs from Mr. Wright. But only the studio retreat, which sits grandly in the Malibu hills, was ever built. Although I photographed it in 1947 for *House and Garden*, Mr. Wright did not have enough new buildings to show from those postwar years, so a planned special issue on him was changed to an article on Taliesin West.

In 1953 at Mr. Wright's request *House and Home* sent me to Phoenix to photograph the newly completed house he had designed for his son David. The house, in the Camelback Mountain district, was built on a flat plot of hard-packed earth cleared for a citrus grove. The house, a new statement by Mr. Wright, was conceived as a complete circle and looked not unlike a coiled rattlesnake poised to strike. It was a challenge to photograph. I worked in a careful, leisurely way, photographing the house from sunup to sundown and from all angles, making sure not to overlook a single nuance.

Mr. Wright wanted to see the black-and-white photographs before I returned to New York so that he would be completely satisfied that I had done a proper job. When I thought that I had finished, I took the proof prints to Mr. Wright. He was pleased. In fact, he was so pleased with one photograph that he said he was tempted to let the magazine have just that one. I knew the magazine would not accept just one photograph, but I also knew that Mr. Wright was not going to insist.

He pored over the photographs, making big OKs or large Xs on the ones he did not want. He took more and more time examining them and seemed to become less and less satisfied.

"What is it that bothers you?" I finally asked him.

"I have a feeling that the house is spinning. We are going to have to anchor it down somehow. You can stick around, can't you?"

"No, sir. I must leave tomorrow. I'm already late."

"Then you may have to come back."

I did not have any idea what Mr. Wright had in mind, but I knew that the magazine would not be happy. *House and Home* never parted easily with its money.

I returned to New York a day or so later and turned over the black-and-white proofs and the color transparencies to the magazine. I was assured that in a few days I would receive a list of the photographs to be used in the layout. The magazine was in a hurry.

Instead, I received a call from *House and Home*. Mr. Wright had wired: "Pete's photographs now obsolete. Send him back."

The magazine responded that it was perfectly satisfied with my photographs and that it was using only ones Mr. Wright had approved.

Mr. Wright wired back: "Photographers waiting in line to redo house—all has changed—send Pete back or forget project."

So I went back. In that short time Mr. Wright had designed and had built a long, straight concrete-block wall five feet high that extended from the house to the street. This was the anchor. Only one photograph or at the most two would tell the story; the other photographs I had taken were unaffected.

I had arranged to meet Mr. Wright at the house. I arrived earlier than he did, so I announced my presence to an amused, surprised David Wright and unpacked and assembled my camera.

Mr. Wright arrived with the sheets of proof prints, which we examined together. I was right. Only one or two views were affected by the change.

"But as long as you're here," he said, "there is something disturbing to me about the way those bougainvilleas fall from the roof terrace." He and I went up to see what was causing the aesthetic static. The bougainvilleas were growing out of two huge wooden planters, one on either side of the window below.

"There's the trouble," he said. "Here, Pete, give me a hand. We'll move these tubs over against the wood. David has them against the concrete. Wood should be against wood."

I was busily tugging at the tubs of plants when David arrived on the scene. He had been attracted from below by

Builder David Henken, the driving force behind the Usonia cooperative in Pleasantville, New York, alerted me one day in 1949 that Mr. Wright was planning to be at the construction site. I grabbed my cameras and drove the twenty miles to be on hand when he arrived. Mr. Wright and Ed Serlin stopped here to study the plans of the house that was to be Serlin's.

100

the wild jerking and swinging of his carefully trained vines.

"What the hell's going on here?"

"Calm down, David. These planters were in the wrong places. Wood against wood—"

"Damn it, Dad. I've worked like hell training those vines."

"Now, now, they'll be much better this way."

"I don't care. I want them where I had them. It's my house."

"Of course, it's your house. But if that's the way you feel about it I'll go."

"Why don't you—and while you're at it, take your photographer with you."

While this dialogue was going on I had been in a position of suspended animation. David's last words shattered me. I had come twenty-five hundred miles to take one photograph and was banished before I could.

"Come on, Pete."

"But—"

As we were leaving through the central garden, Mr. Wright paused under the overhead ramp. Squatting slightly he described a view through a rough square made by his thumbs and index fingers. "Take this," he said, "if David will let you."

At this point the whole thing struck me as very funny, but we beat a hasty retreat with David standing by, glaring at us. I walked Mr. Wright to his car, where one of his apprentices, Richard Carney, now the managing trustee of the Frank Lloyd Wright Foundation, was waiting. After filling two bushel baskets with grapefruit from David's orchard, Mr. Wright took off.

I was completely frustrated. I stood by my car and wondered how to approach a justifiably angry David. In a short while he came to where I was standing and explained that he had not really meant to take it out on me but that he could not back down now. He said, "Please try to under-

stand that if I let Dad win this one I will never win another one." He was sorry; he knew I had come a long way.

But there was nothing to prevent me from taking a photograph of the house from the road. And that I did. The resulting photograph made a beautiful opening page for the *House and Home* story.

Much of my work for Mr. Wright in the 1950s was done around New York City, except for the Neils house in Minneapolis, which I photographed in October 1952. In the late 1940s and early 1950s Mr. Wright's time was taken up with visits to Usonia in Pleasantville, New York, where he had designed three houses: the Friedman house, which I did not photograph until long after Mr. Wright had died; the Serlin house, which was altered by another architect and to my mind no longer deserved to be called Wright's; and the Reisley house, which I photographed under construction and at various times when Mr. Wright was checking on its progress.

Early in the spring of 1958 I received a telephone call from Mr. Wright. He announced that he was in New Canaan, Connecticut, visiting Joyce and John Rayward, for whom he had designed a house, and he invited me to meet him there for lunch. I joined the group as they were finishing and was pleased to see Mr. Wright looking so well. We talked, drank coffee, and were strolling around the grounds when Mr. Wright suddenly declared that he would like to pay a visit to his old friend Philip Johnson, the architect, who also lived in New Canaan. Besides, he had never seen Johnson's widely publicized Glass House. A call was made. Johnson was in and would be delighted to have us come over right away.

The day, although overcast, was bright and shadowless. Moisture from recent showers intensified the stark color of the setting—the brilliant green of the perfectly

New Canaan, Connecticut, is a town of mainly colonial homes, some of them genuine. But many of America's foremost architects—Marcel Breuer, Philip Johnson, Edward Durell Stone, Elliott Noyes, and Frank Lloyd Wright— also have left their imprints in town. In the mid-1950s Mr. Wright designed a house there for the Raywards. Called Tirranna ("running waters"), it sits on the edge of a pond. Like other Wright designs of this period, the house was built of concrete block on a circular module.

manicured lawn, the tender yellow-green of the newly sprouted leaves against the black trunks of recently dormant trees. We walked single file, Mr. Wright heading the procession on a white pebble path so bright it hurt our eyes.

The Johnson house, a nearly perfect box of glass, acted as both a window and a mirror. It seemed a surrealistic stage for an unbelievable drama. But then we had an unbelievable cast.

Philip Johnson appeared from behind a solid wood door and extended his hand to Mr. Wright.

"Welcome to the monkey house!" he said.

"But why 'monkey house?'" asked Mr. Wright.

"That's what you called it," was the reply.

"Now, now, Philip, I said nothing of the kind. I merely said that you were quite capable of designing one, not that you had." Then he asked, "Philip, do you know all these people?"

After some congenial amenities the afternoon settled down to ample Scotch and a three-way discussion of the history of architecture. Johnson had a guest of his own that day, Alfred Barr, director of the Museum of Modern Art. The three men kept the air alive with their philosophical differences. Johnson, still riding a high crest of public adulation over his triumph as collaborator with Ludwig Mies van der Rohe on the Seagram Building in New York City, was proud and expansive. Mr. Wright was friendly and indulgent. Good-natured jibes were batted back and forth, and then the conversation gave way to a lecture on the birth of architecture and how far it had come, delivered by the inimitable Frank Lloyd Wright. In that antihouse—the perfect stage for that drama—we were as raptly involved in the demonstration as if we had been watching an intense theatrical production.

At the time Mr. Wright was bringing his own genius to New York City. The Guggenheim Museum was wind-

ing its way upward against its perpendicular backdrop on Fifth Avenue. The contrast between the Seagram and the Guggenheim buildings piqued Mr. Wright into an illustrated lesson on the history of architecture going back, it seemed, to beyond the caves. Crayon in hand and using a large drawing pad on Johnson's table, he guided us from the early use of bamboo to marble to steel. He demonstrated how the fluted columns of the Parthenon were but stylized carvings in marble of clusters of bamboo bound together with ropes of vines. He talked on and on, pausing only to replenish his Scotch.

In the very center of one end of the living room, grandly placed on a large pedestal, was a model of one of Elie Nadelman's figures that adorn the lobby of Lincoln Center's New York State Theater, which Johnson had designed. The placement of the piece obviously annoyed Mr. Wright, a notorious furniture arranger, for in the middle of his illustrated tirade, Scotch in hand, he pushed the statue and pedestal off center. Although appearing not to notice, Johnson pushed the figure back into position as soon as he could. This went on through the hour or so that we were in the conversationalists' thrall. Finally, having held forth for a very long time on the failure of modern architects to use steel in a new and daring fashion, Mr. Wright concluded his lecture with the perfect example: a detailed drawing of what looked suspiciously like the Seagram Building. Just as he was about to toss down the crayon and bow to the applause, he caught sight of Johnson returning the statue once again to dead center.

With obvious impatience he declared, "Philip, such symmetry is reserved only for God."

It was time to go. I regret that I had neither my camera nor a tape recorder to capture the drama of that magic afternoon. And I have often wondered what—or who—Mr. Wright had in mind when he alluded to perfect symmetry and to God.

The Jacobs house in Madison, Wisconsin—the first Usonian, built 1936–37—was my first photo assignment away from the Taliesins. He was with me, he got me started, and he told me what he wanted documented. After warnings about what he did not want in the photographs, Mr. Wright went off to other chores and came back to pick me up in the afternoon. The results pleased him—now I could be sent to shoot his work without the master's supervision.

104

Another of the first projects Mr. Wright entrusted to me during my first summer at Taliesin in 1940 was the Schwartz house in Two Rivers, Wisconsin. It grew out of a prototype he published in *Life* magazine in 1938, a house "For a Family of $5,000–$6,000 Income." Of the actual shooting I remember little except that Schwartz rowed me out to the middle of a lake and showed me his favorite view of the house. From that time on I always forswore night shots from a rowboat.

The Pew house in
Madison, Wisconsin,
was not completed
when I photographed
it in the summer of
1940, but Mr. Wright
wanted it in the   108
MoMA exhibit.   ■
                        ■
                        ■
                        ■
                        ■

Built of limestone and
cypress with dramatic
overhangs, the Pew
house hugs the shore
of Lake Mendota,
providing views as
well as privacy among
the trees.

Mr. Wright enthusiastically embraced even the most difficult site. Most architects and builders would have tried to avoid this hilly challenge in Brentwood Heights, California. Instead, Mr. Wright in 1939 cantilevered over the problem. The Sturges house, in spite of its dramatic visibility from all angles, has always been extremely private. These exterior and interior views date from 1947, when I shot them for a *House and Garden* feature.

My experience in meeting Mr. Wright's exacting needs had prepared me well for photographing the Pauson house in Phoenix. He was too busy to visit the site and left it entirely for me to shoot as I saw fit. Mr. Wright was delighted with the images.

But it had been an easy task. Rose Pauson appreciated what Mr. Wright had created for her and minimized her own touches. I did not have to move a thing.

The Pauson house dominated a gentle mound covered with stone rubble and desert flora. I photographed it from all angles and from various distances. From several points it looked like a ship riding out a swelling wave. It was a starkly beautiful and simple statement designed around the techniques Mr. Wright developed at Taliesin West.

As I was photographing the Pauson house, I was preparing myself psychologically for a separation from the Fellowship and Mr. Wright. The year was 1941, and I had been warned that I was about to be drafted. I had to tell Mr. Wright that I was going to join some branch of the military to meet my father's wishes, which was against Mr. Wright's own advice. I did not anticipate an easy time of this, so I outdid myself hoping to dazzle him with the photographs. The Pauson house was my last assignment as a Wright apprentice.

The house accidentally burned in 1941. Rose Pauson chose not to rebuild.

The rubblestone walls and foundations of the ruin, known as Ship Rock, thereafter served as a notorious trysting place for a generation of local teenagers and an eerie ruin in the desert.

Before the city bulldozed 32nd Street through the remains in the 1980s one sentimental (or enterprising) person had the huge south chimney moved to serve as a landmark for a new housing development nearby.

One photograph I took of the Pauson house illustrates the flaw that caused the fire: the huge French doors left ajar allowed a night breeze to blow the curtain against the embers in the fireplace. Unfortunately, the superstructure of the house was redwood and was totally consumed, leaving only the base of desert stone and concrete.

In the summer of 1947 Mr. Wright called and asked me to drive to Lakeland, Florida, to photograph his latest work: three new buildings at Florida Southern College (the Pfeiffer Chapel is at left).

"Your expenses will be paid by the college, and the Museum of Modern Art will buy some photographs from you. You should come out all right," he instructed.

I was housed, gratis, in an empty girls' dormitory. The Wright apprentices supervising the project were Kenn Lockhart and his wife, Polly (now Frances Nemtin). I had my meals with them, so my expenses, as Mr. Wright had foreseen, were minimal. I had continued my involvement with Mr. Wright and Taliesin since I had returned from the war, but this was my first encounter with an apprentice and friend, working and living away from Taliesin.

When I finished the job and returned to New York City, I took the proofs to MoMA, where, I was sure, I would reap a small fortune. The museum loved the prints but purchased only one — its budget allowed just $1.50 for an 8-by-10-inch print. So, after 2,000 miles, a week's travel, four days of photography, and two days in the laboratory, I had a $1.50 print order. I was stunned.

I thought that perhaps "Architectural Forum" might be interested in seeing my proofs. I was right. "Forum" was working on a 1948 issue devoted to Mr. Wright's work. But Mr. Wright insisted that the magazine use only drawings, no photographs. After seeing my images, Paul Grotz, the editor, decided to try to persuade Mr. Wright one more time to use photographs. He called Mr. Wright while I was still in his office. "Okay, Paul," he said. "Have Pete come down and bring everything he has."

"Forum" won out, and the 1948 issue contained photographs. But it might not have if MoMA had bought more prints. And Mr. Wright sneaked in his drawings: he "planted" leaves on this view to make it seem less bare, and that is the view that "Forum" ran.

Whenever possible Mr. Wright would accompany me on a shoot. Going along afforded him the opportunity to visit one of his houses and harrumph over offending accessories added by the owner.

He would illustrate to me what he would not accept under any circumstances: no pictures of Grandpa, no photographs on the piano, no pastel renderings of children, no matter how cute. His opinions could be brutal.

He declared that I should destroy, if I thought I could get away with it, any of these unauthorized accessories.

In 1948 I visited Taliesin to show Mr. Wright some photographs, including a portrait of him. While I was there he decided to take advantage of the opportunity and asked me to photograph the Unitarian Meeting House in Madison, Wisconsin.

In an extreme example of his penchant for purity, he ordered me to pull down every third panel of the immense draperies at the church. He thought that when the curtains were open they bunched up excessively against the stone walls.

"Should I," I asked, "put them back up when I'm through photographing?" It would be a monumental task.

"No," he said, "take them outside and burn them."

It did not matter that when closed the draperies would not cover the windows. I did not put them back, nor did I burn them. I folded them as neatly as I could and left them stacked behind the receptionist's desk.

After another tour of the place to see that I would leave nothing unphotographed, Mr. Wright took off. As he left I heard him humming a tune from an old stage musical, the words to which went, "Every little movement has a meaning all its own." The Wright philosophy surely.

Never missing a forum
in which to talk about
his work, Mr. Wright
went on the "Today"
show in 1953 and
explained organic
architecture to host
Hugh Downs and vast
numbers of viewers.
The triangular form of
the Unitarian Meeting
House, announced
Mr. Wright, embodied
aspiration and an all-
encompassing unity
that was right for the
Unitarians, of which
he was one. The
upward sweep of the
roof, he added, "says
what the steeple used
to say, but says it with
greater reverence,
I think, in both form
and structure."

Mr. Wright made many visits to the Usonia site in Pleasantville, New York. Here he and builder David Henken, a former apprentice, review the plans for the Reisley house on its wooded terrain in 1949. After the house, the last of three at Usonia, was finished he came again in 1952 (opposite) to address the problem of a chimney that was not drawing properly— quickly and authoritatively sketching out his ideas (including a new fireplace grate).

Mr. Wright developed the site plan for Usonia, but he designed only three of the planned fifty-five houses. David Henken also designed a number of houses in Usonia, including one for himself. Mr. Wright took advantage of his 1949 inspection tour of the project to stop and offer advice to Henken. With Mr. Wright here are Henken, Robert Chuckrow, John Peter, an editor at *Look* magazine, and Anne Peter. Mr. Wright (opposite) pondered another problem with architect Aaron Resnick, who designed this and other houses at Usonia.

In October 1952 as I finished my latest stint at Taliesin, Mr. Wright directed me to Minneapolis to photograph the recently completed Neils house. Neils, owner of the Flour City Ornamental Marble Works, wanted a design using culled marble from his marble business. Mr. Wright complied, and thirty varieties of marble were used.

David Wright allowed me to take only two photographs of his Phoenix house after he and his father had their little tiff about moving the bougain-villeas. The view of the five-foot-high wall extending from the street to the house (opposite) was one of them. It made a fine opening to the story in the June 1953 *House and Home*. I had a chance to photograph it again, from the air, in March 1959 on my last assignment for Mr. Wright.

The exterior curves of
David Wright's house
are mirrored inside in
features such as the
living room fireplace
and the furnishings.

"This is the essence of the house. We don't need any others," Mr. Wright told me. *House and Home* thought otherwise.

Shortly after Mr. Wright died in 1959, the architecture magazines feverishly began publishing stories on his work. *Architectural Forum* used a number of my photographs to accompany articles on Mr. Wright and sent me to Bethesda, Maryland, to photograph the house of Robert Llewelyn Wright, his son. I was on a limited budget and short of time— I had just a day to photograph it and another to process the film to meet a deadline. Designed in 1953 the house was landscaped in 1960 by Robert's brother Lloyd Wright.

I shot Beth Sholom
Synagogue in Elkins
Park, Pennsylvania,
shortly after Mr. Wright   134
died but before it   ■
was finished.   ■
                            ■
                            ■
                            ■

Later, in 1960, after
Beth Sholom was
dedicated I returned
to complete the docu-
mentation, also for
Architectural Forum.

TALIESIN EAST

In the 1950s Mr. Wright took up temporary residence in New York City so that he could lend his watchful eye to projects such as a retrospective exhibition of his work at the site of the future Solomon R. Guggenheim Museum as well as the museum itself.

His arrival was like the coming of the circus. Everyone was watching him and listening to him. He was filmed on the exhibition site daily and was constantly interviewed by the press, radio, and television. He was a frequent guest on the "Today" show. At that time the program was televised on the ground floor of one of the Rockefeller Center buildings and could be observed through a big window by people on their way to work. Mr. Wright, an early riser and dedicated walker, often stopped to watch as he passed the window.

The Plaza was Mr. Wright's favorite New York hotel. In 1953, as the retrospective exhibition was ending and planning for the Guggenheim Museum construction began, he arranged with Harry Guggenheim to secure a permanent home and office at the Plaza. Suite 223 became known as Taliesin East.

Here Mr. Wright held court, entertaining contractors, admirers, and would-be clients such as Marilyn Monroe. It offered him a base close to the Guggenheim site and the midtown Manhattan area he covered in his daily walks.

My greatest involvement with Mr. Wright at this time was during the construction of the Usonian model house and the pavilion for his Sixty Years of Living Architecture exhibition (November 22, 1953, to January 16, 1954), which was subtitled In the Realm of Ideas. This show, installed on the Guggenheim site, had opened in Philadelphia in 1951 and then traveled around the world. The retrospective exhibition was so popular that it was extended beyond its planned closing date. Los Angeles got to see it after its run in New York.

The largest exhibit to date of Mr. Wright's designs, it also involved the largest Fellowship effort away from either of the Taliesins. Fourteen apprentices came from Wisconsin and spent the better part of the summer and fall of 1953 constructing a two-bedroom Usonian house, which was to be the major focus of the exhibit and the first Wright structure built in the city. Next to it was constructed a huge pavilion to house Mr. Wright's models and drawings as well as photographs, many of which were mine. John Geiger, who had been a Taliesin apprentice since 1947, supervised the work.

David Henken, himself a former apprentice, had contracted to build the exhibit structure. We had been good friends since 1948. Through him and Mr. Wright, who was on hand nearly every day, I had entrée to the site to photograph the project from start to finish.

With Mr. Wright's required piano installed, the 1953 exhibition pavilion was ready to open in New York. There was no apparent reason for the piano: no performances were scheduled. Only when the exhibition was not crowded did Mr. Wright sit and run through his obligatory bars of Beethoven or Bach. Toward the end of the show Mr. Wright sent for a truck from Taliesin to take the piano back there. But the lender, Steinway and Sons, got wind of Mr. Wright's intentions and rescued the piano.

While Mr. Wright was breaking new ground in New York City, he was also doing battle with another famous egotist: Robert Moses, New York's commissioner of public works. Moses had the authority to approve or waive every statute or code governing construction in the city, safety being paramount. The exhibition pavilion was designed to be built almost like a roofed-over scaffold, a greenhouse-like structure smack among the mansions and elite apartments on Fifth Avenue. At every turn Moses questioned Mr. Wright's designs and materials. The battle of the egos went on, accounts sometimes spilling into the daily press and other times just trickling down among us from Mr. Wright himself. Mr. Wright and Moses came out of the many frays good friends, even claiming to be distant cousins through marriage.

At age eighty-six Mr. Wright still turned many heads and commanded a league of admirers. Those of us who were working at the exhibition site became accustomed to seeing an elderly woman appear at the site every day at about the same time and watch with extraordinary interest for long periods. One day she engaged David Henken in conversation. She was a long-time admirer of Mr. Wright, she confessed, and had unsuccessfully invested much of her time in recent days trying to catch a glimpse of him.

"Is he present now?" she wanted to know. By this time the place was being closed in, and one could not see the entire project as before. Henken replied that, as a matter of fact, he was. Would she care to meet him? "Oh, my, yes," she said, "but he wouldn't—"

Henken was already explaining the situation to Mr. Wright, who had been going over progress reports. He returned with Henken to be introduced to his admirer. After introductions and the proper compliments and acknowledgments, Mr. Wright asked the woman if she would like to see what he was doing. She would.

"Then take my arm and come with me," he said. And with her arm in his, they stepped over boards and ducked under trusses as they disappeared into the gaping beehive. After this day she was never seen at the site again, and we were left to romanticize as to her feelings about having walked arm-in-arm with her hero of fifty years.

Mr. Wright often arrived at the exhibition site by taxi and penniless. I came up with some money when I saw him vainly going through his pockets. Much has been written about Mr. Wright and his creditors, but I saw no evidence of his neglecting to repay debts. At an age when he could be forgiven for forgetting a $1.50 taxi fare, he never did. It might be hours or even days later, but he would always say, "Oh, here, Pete, I owe you for the taxi."

Another day, after one appearance on the "Today" show, Mr. Wright stopped for breakfast at a counter-service luncheonette catering to the quick-turnover customer. He ordered and ate the eighty-five-cent special and then discovered, on reaching into his pocket, that he had no money. Consternation was followed by the waitress and then the manager, who, recognizing Mr. Wright, offered to parole him on his own recognizance if he would simply sign the back of the check, which he did.

Later that morning Mr. Wright returned and asked to see the manager.

"I believe I owe you eighty-five cents."

"Oh no, Mr. Wright, my treat."

"No, no, right is right."

"But I insist."

"No, bring me the check."

The manager reluctantly handed Mr. Wright the sales slip, and Mr. Wright gave him eighty-five cents.

"If it's my autograph you want, eighty-five cents isn't the going rate. I hear that it brings at least five dollars now."

Mr. Wright's extended visits to New York City created many opportunities for television, radio, and newspapers. He posed for professionals and amateurs alike. He became so used to having cameras thrust in his face that he grew oblivious of their presence, as one can see here. The boy at left is Brandock Peters, son of Wes Peters and Mrs. Wright's daughter Svetlana.

139

During this time, knowing that Mr. Wright was fond of Mexican food, I wrote to my mother asking her to prepare and arrange to serve a Mexican lunch at Taliesin West when the Wrights were in residence. This was not an undue burden on my mother; my father was a partner in a Mexican food processing company, which would make available to her all the components of the lunch and any personnel she might need. Mother's role would be supervisory; she would naturally serve as hostess. Afterward Mother wrote me that the luncheon had gone well.

Her letter came at the same time that the Wrights arrived back in New York City on business. Ben Raeburn of Horizon Press, Mr. Wright's publisher, and I went to the Plaza Hotel to shoot some photographs. After setting up the lights and camera, I began photographing Mr. Wright. We were almost finished with our work when a door opened behind me. It was Mrs. Wright. I had to turn around to see her.

Ignoring my presence for the moment, she said firmly, "Frank, come to bed—you need your rest."

"We're almost through, Olga," Mr. Wright responded. "We'll only be another minute."

"No," she said. "I want you to come right now. You are going out tonight, and you need to rest."

I stood there waiting for the chance to greet her properly, but she went on.

"Just come, Frank. Pedro can come back tomorrow." And with that our eyes met.

"Good evening, Mrs. Wright," I said.

"Well, Pedro," she said. "I had lunch with your mother last week."

"I know. She wrote me about it."

"She is a charming woman."

"Thank you," I responded. "I'll write and tell her you said so. She'll be very pleased."

"Too bad," she said, receding into the bedroom and closing the door behind her, "that none of that charm rubbed off on you."

Mr. Wright only smiled and looked at me with what I interpreted as sympathy. We finished the assignment. Only then did Mr. Wright go off for his nap. I packed my gear and left.

This episode involving Mrs. Wright was not the first time she had expressed displeasure with my "character," but it was one of the most public upbraidings. If she had ever discussed the problem with Mr. Wright, it had not affected my relationship with him: once when she had been critical of me in his presence, he chided her by saying: "Now, now, mother. Go easy on Pete. He's a good boy." When I called after this latest incident, my mother told me that Mrs. Wright had complained to her that I had become a sophisticated New Yorker and that she had been much fonder of me before.

Mrs. Wright had previously singled me out to be lectured on various subjects, among them my poor manners and the law of retribution. On the evening of the dedication of the Guggenheim retrospective she took me aside and railed at me unmercifully. I did not know what my offense had been, but I was quite impressed with my sudden celebrity. I was sure that the arriving company must have thought I was someone important to be so thoroughly savaged by the hostess.

I continued to visit Mr. Wright at the Plaza. Once on a purely social occasion things went very well between Mrs. Wright and me, perhaps because I had the good sense to bring her a gigantic bouquet of rust-colored chrysanthemums from my garden. The fact that she was swayed into graciousness by my simple gift gave me a clue. She evidently believed that I was not paying her the respect she felt she deserved as Mr. Wright grew older. I believe now that she was beginning to establish her own power base, for if she was going to survive after Mr. Wright's death, she had to take control. And in fact some of us were never invited back to Taliesin from the time Mr. Wright died until after her own death in 1985, a period of twenty-six years.

Mrs. Wright had taken excellent care of Mr. Wright for three decades and deserved the gratitude of all of us in the Fellowship, past and present. Gratitude, but not tribute. Perhaps in the end it is just as well that I did not seek her approval. My admiration and my loyalty were to him alone.

While the 1953 retrospective exhibition was considered a huge success, the Usonian house itself was trouble from the beginning. The whole project ran over budget and behind schedule. After the exhibition Mr. Wright decided to auction off the model. It sold with his proviso that the buyer have David Henken, the original builder, supervise its reconstruction. The house sold quickly at auction, but the buyer contracted polio soon thereafter and realized that he would not be able to adapt the house to his new condition. The disassembled house had been stored in Henken's basement workshop, so it was logical that he purchase it in the hope of finding another buyer. It lay there for twenty-nine years, all but forgotten.

In May 1984 Scott Elliott of the Kelmscott Gallery in Chicago, learning of the house's existence, persuaded Henken to offer it to Channel 13, the New York City PBS affiliate, for its fund-raising auction. Channel 13 jumped at the chance. A reserve price of $50,000 was set; one stipulation was that another $50,000 would be paid to Henken for supervising the house's rebuilding.

Word went out about this once-in-a-lifetime sale. Bids came in from all over the United States and from Europe and Japan. Tom Monaghan, the pizza mogul and collector of Wrightiana, won with a bid of $117,000.

Elliott, who had been out of the country, was stunned that neither he nor his gallery was identified with the auction, and he mistakenly blamed Henken for this.

After twenty-nine years the house had been reduced to a bundle of sticks. A number of pieces were missing, but it was trucked off to Monaghan's headquarters in Ann Arbor, Michigan. After six months of discussions with an officer of Monaghan's organization who questioned the need for Henken's services, Henken flew to Ann Arbor for a Monday morning appointment with Monaghan. On Sunday he was shown the proposed site of the house by Lawrence Brink, Monaghan's architecture adviser and a former Wright apprentice. The next morning Brink arrived at Henken's hotel and called his room from the lobby. Henken announced that he would be right down. As he approached the car, he collapsed and died of a heart attack, a few weeks shy of his sixty-ninth birthday.

On March 17, 1992, while visiting the Leslie Hindman auction gallery in Chicago, where some of my Wright photographs were consigned for auction, I recognized a familiar collection of artifacts: the bundle of sticks that had once been the Usonian model. Monaghan had donated it to the Frank Lloyd Wright Building Conservancy, which determined that the house could not be restored and opted to auction it once more, but this time just for its parts. Little of it sold. Among the few pieces that did sell were three clerestory panels, two of which I had once owned, having bought them in the late 1950s from Henken for three dollars each. I had hinged them together and used them as a screen to hide the back of my piano; I later sold them because they had been damaged in the fire that destroyed my home and took my wife's life.

The pathetic mound of wooden panels, doors, and hardware at the auction was the last public view of a star-crossed house.

As soon as he moved into his Plaza suite, Mr. Wright began to change it to suit his needs. First it needed a piano and then "the necessities": a red and black lacquer desk and other furniture of his own design, much of it made by the apprentices. He embellished the Beaux Arts windows with round mirrors encircled with wooden borders painted Cherokee red. Gold-toned wallpaper and thick peach-colored carpet were added. In typical Wright fashion the only adornment in his office was a portrait of his mother and a dazzling painting by Georgia O'Keeffe, a gift from her.

Mr. Wright was always on hand at the site of his 1953 retrospective exhibition in New York City to solve construction problems as they arose. Here he reviews plans with David Henken, contractor for the Usonian model house, the centerpiece of the show.

Either with a wave of his cane or a few well-directed words, Mr. Wright would explain what had to be done next. When, many years later, Michael Zingg of Madison, Wisconsin, saw the photograph shown here, he said, "For myself, it goes beyond a simple workman trying to grasp and understand Mr. Wright. That worker is all of us struggling with his ideas, with a new order, struggling in the end with the genius of the man himself."

AND THOU, AMERICA . . . .

Thou, too, surroundest all,
Embracing, carrying, welcoming all, thou too
By pathways broad and new approach the Ideal.

The measured faiths of other lands,
The grandeurs of the past, are not for thee,
But grandeurs of thine own,
Deific faiths and amplitudes, absorbing, comprehending all,
All in all to all.

Give me, O God, to sing that thought,
Give me, give him or her I love this quenchless faith in Thee.
Whatever else withheld withhold not from us
Belief in plan of Thee enclosed in Time and Space . . . .

Fragment transcribed from Walt Whitman

REALM OF IDEAS
TO YOU . . . THIS RECORD OF PATIENT
RESEARCH AND GENUINE EXPERIMENT
ACCORDING TO EXPERIENCE FAITHFUL
TO THE NATURE OF WHATEVER WAS
BEING DONE

A portrait of Mr. Wright standing at his Taliesin drafting table, one of my photographs, greeted visitors as they entered the exhibition pavilion. Mr. Wright had cropped this photograph at the level of the drafting board—to my vigorous protest. He responded: "I wanted the photograph to say, 'I am an architect—what'll you have?'" What could I say?

Walking through the retrospective exhibition, I came upon Mr. Wright having a tea break. It was a scene so perfect that it could not have been planned. There he was, with his porkpie hat, stiff collar, and cane, sitting before a selection of his favorite architecture: the San Francisco Call Building model and photo murals of the Larkin Building in Buffalo. The same day (opposite) he paused before a model of Wingspread. I had an assignment from the Ford Motor Company to shoot a portrait of him—but I did not have to pose him even for this one.

Something of an
anomaly in its neigh-
borhood—the site of
the Guggenheim—
Mr. Wright's Usonian   150
exhibition house   ■
opened in 1953.   ■
                              ■
                              ■
                              ■

Furniture for the house
was designed on the
spot by Mr. Wright.
Paul Bechtal, a Long
151   Island cabinet maker,
■   was assigned the task
■   of building it.
·
·
■

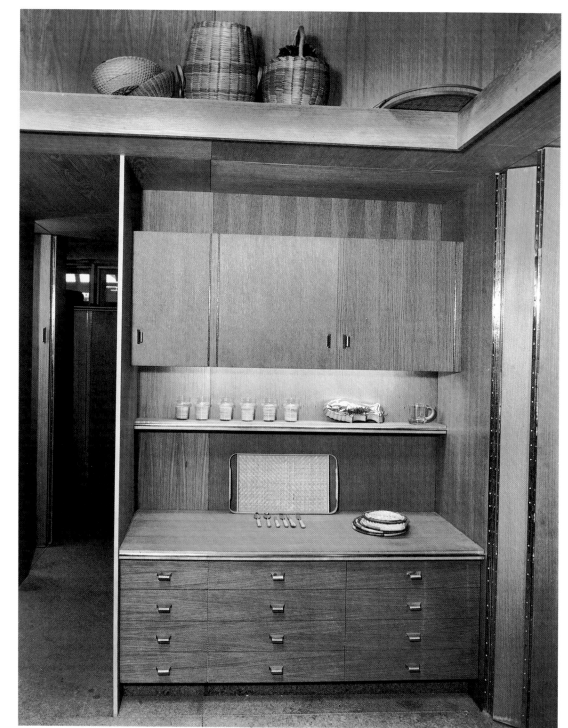

Plans for the house and its furnishings began as a rough sketch that Mr. Wright handed to David Henken, the builder. Henken needed no more direction than that to proceed with construction. Because the house was meant to be temporary, it had no foundation and rose directly from an asphalt slab.

As the house progressed and the carpenters reached an undefined area of construction, Henken and Mr. Wright would huddle over a drawing and together would plot the next move. There was little about the house that could be solved by simply sending someone to a lumber yard. Only the plumbing came ready made.

154

The entire effort to build the temporary Usonian model as part of the Wright retrospective exhibition was a "solve-as-we-go-along" project. This method was not only inefficient; it was also expensive, so the house began to fall behind schedule and over budget. To save the day, Mr. Wright brought in apprentices from Wisconsin to help finish it. With this nearly free labor, the budget held.

Ben Raeburn of Horizon Press, the publisher of Mr. Wright's forthcoming book "The Future of Architecture," alerted me in 1953 to be prepared to photograph Mr. Wright in New York.

During a television interview with Hugh Downs on the "Today" show some months earlier, he had demonstrated with his hands the differences between organic and conventional architecture. Raeburn wanted to use the series to accompany the complete text of Mr. Wright's conversation in the book. There was no videotape then to capture the event, so Raeburn needed reenactments of each technique as illustrations.

I met him at Mr. Wright's suite at the Plaza Hotel, and step by step we recreated the television lesson. The resulting twelve images are shown at right. In the first six photos Mr. Wright illustrated conventional architecture and its use of post-and-beam construction: (1) posts and beams, (2) beams and posts, (3) cutting and slashing partitions, (4) butting partitions, (5) riveting to make a connection and create tension, and (6) how the rivet might give way because of the rigidness of conventional architecture.

In the next series (views 7 through 10) Mr. Wright clasped his hands together, interlocking his fingers to indicate the strength and flexibility of his organic architecture. As he talked he rocked his hands back and forth, showing how organic architecture had a tensile strength because it could use steel to span great spaces. In organic architecture, he said, "You see one thing merging into another and being of another rather than this old cut, butt and slash."

In the last two photographs Mr. Wright explained his design concept for the Unitarian Meeting House in Madison, Wisconsin, finished a while earlier. The plan was triangular, as he showed, and the roof, illustrated by placing his hands together, also was triangular. The shape created the "expression of reverence without recourse to the steeple," he modestly explained.

AU REVOIR

In January 1959, when I was photographing Mr. Wright's suite at the Plaza Hotel in New York City, we discussed Taliesin West. I had last seen it in 1953, when I had been in Arizona to photograph David Wright's house.

"It has been too long," Mr. Wright declared. "We have made many changes. Why don't you plan on coming in the spring—redo the whole camp, photograph the changes. When did you join us?"

"In 1939," I replied.

"Then we will call it Taliesin Revisited. Call me when you are ready. We'll pick up your expenses."

And so early in March 1959 I flew to Arizona, summoned by the master.

It had been a long time, and there were many changes. Travelers no longer generated a plume of dust for the entire trip to Taliesin West. The road was now "improved"—dressed with culverts and paved. Within sight of Taliesin West were newly constructed houses, and large subdivisions extended for miles. Scottsdale was no longer a cow town but a fast-growing resort community with all its attendant vulgar boutiques.

Even Taliesin West itself had changed. A wide, straight unpaved road now ran parallel to the main structure, and a handsome, triumphant pillar greeted me from the orderly parking area. I could see immediately that much had been added since my last visit, such as a dance pavilion and several other structures. Mr. Wright's personal studio and office was unchanged, except that now telephones had been installed. One new person, a young woman with unusually heavy rouge and lipstick, sat at the telephone and answered it with a very professional "Taliesin West."

I could see Gene Masselink hovering beyond the young woman, and I made my presence known to him with a wave of the hand. After a genial greeting, he informed me that Mr. Wright was in the drafting room.

The room was a study in concentration. Almost all the tables were in use, some with two or three persons involved on one problem. In every group of two or more, I recognized a familiar face. Mr. Wright was engrossed at the north end of the room, going over some engineering details with Wes Peters.

Heads rose slowly as I entered, but the hush that pervaded the room persisted. Those who knew me acknowledged my presence with a nod of the head or a silent hello but no sound. One of them finally rose, came to me, and with a quiet handshake and whisper asked what I was doing there.

"Mr. Wright sent for me," I answered.

"He's very busy at the moment. If I were you I wouldn't disturb him. Why don't you look around for a half hour or so?"

159

When I revisited Taliesin West in March 1959 Mr. Wright was mellower. He made himself available to me, and he did not beg off or question the need for yet another portrait. He even suggested that I photograph him with Mrs. Wright, something he had not requested before. This was my last portrait of him alone.

Mr. Wright did, in fact, look most involved, and by Wes's furrowed brow I could tell it was important. However, I knew he must consider my being there important too. Otherwise, why would he have sent for me?

So, in turning to leave, I was deliberately clumsy and bumped into a blueprint case, making enough of a sound to arouse Mr. Wright. Seeing me standing there, he threw down his pencil.

"Well, Pete, you're here. Good! You couldn't have arrived at a better time. I need to take a walk."

He rose. We shook hands and left the drafting room together. I did not look back to see how many were offended by my intrusion—or how many were pleased that I was taking Mr. Wright away.

We circled the entire compound, Mr. Wright guiding me to a starting point at the new road and then shortcutting through the rough, untrammeled desert to the apprentices' quarters. It was the same sort of walk we had taken together years before.

I was astounded at the vigor in his stride. Only a few months from his ninety-second birthday, he was erect and alert. As we walked he talked about many things: color, texture, light and form, the encroachment of civilization on the desert. In the old familiar way he pointed his cane at little things that amused or pleased him: a delicately beautiful desert flower, a shy bird or animal. He talked about the obvious changes that had taken place during my absence and pointed out what areas and vistas needed rephotographing. After a time—it might have been more than half an hour—he left me. I always felt privileged and enriched by the time I spent in his presence, no matter how short, particularly when we were alone together. This was where it had all started. I was back home.

I was to do a complete photographic study of Taliesin West again. There were, of course, incongruities. The so-

phisticated tent with its roof flaps up to catch cool breezes had been made fast. Glass was now permanently fixed in areas that had once been open to nature. In one or two small rooms electric heaters and air conditioners were evident. I puzzled over this. Remembering the beauty of the simple statement Taliesin West made in 1940 I was disappointed. And yet things have to change. A structure used as a workshop and a habitation has to evolve to remain alive. The experiment I had been part of near its beginning was not over.

The Fellowship activity was basically the same but with a new pull and involvement. After lunch the dance pavilion became the center of activity. Under the aegis and supervision of Mrs. Wright, a former dancer and long a disciple of the French-Russian mystic Gurdjieff, the white-clad apprentices rehearsed a series of dance steps and body movements for an hour or so in the afternoon.

I entered the pavilion for a short rest and to catch a little of the rehearsal. There was another spectator there—a businessman from Michigan at Taliesin West for a conference with Mr. Wright regarding the possibility of a million-dollar commission.

"Does this go on all the time?" he asked me.

"I think so—for a time in the afternoon, anyway."

"Good God, the man is over ninety. These people are his draftsmen. There must be hundreds of projects they should be working on. But dancing? They will never get to me."

That unfortunate man had arrived shortly before noon. Mr. Wright usually napped after lunch and did not surface again until about three o'clock. He had no choice but to wait and fret, which he did. But his grand plans, whatever they were, were not to include Mr. Wright.

While I was at Taliesin West, I read in the local newspaper that the first Mrs. Wright had died. The notice was a very small item at the bottom of an inside page. I asked Mr. Wright about her when I saw him next.

"She was a very lovely person," he said. "She lived a long time."

That was all he said.

After he died, a short time later, I romanticized that he had paced himself with her and realized his own mortality.

The Sunday before I left Taliesin West I attended a formal dinner, starting with cocktails for the senior apprentices in the living room. I was the first to arrive and busied myself walking around and taking notice of the changes in that lovely room. Mrs. Wright came in, looking upset.

"Pedro, have you seen Mr. Wright?"

"No, Mrs. Wright, I haven't."

"This is very unusual. He is always the first one here. I can't find him. Would you look for him, please?"

"Of course."

I did not have to look far. I found Mr. Wright asleep on one of the long built-in seats before the huge fireplace in the cove. I woke him.

"I'll be right witcha," he said as he swung his feet to the floor. As he took my arm he said, "I talk more and more like a gangster as I get older."

He had, I gathered, never disappeared like this before. Mrs. Wright was relieved to see him but obviously concerned about this unusual behavior. The party started then, and I thought no more about the incident.

The next morning I photographed Mr. Wright alone in his studio and that afternoon Mr. and Mrs. Wright together in the living room. Neither shooting was as successful as I had expected, a fact that has disturbed me greatly since.

I left Arizona on March 14 to process the photographs I had just taken. I interrupted the work to fulfill an assignment in Delaware for the *Ladies' Home Journal,* and it was there that I received word that Mr. Wright had died on April 9. The news was a shock for me. It had been only a little more than three weeks since we had taken a stroll through the desert. He seemed indestructible then. I thought he would live forever.

After tea in the garden room at Taliesin West, Mrs. Wright reads from Aldous Huxley's *Brave New World*. This was to be their last sitting together for me. Mr. Wright did not live to see the finished prints. Even while taking these images I was not aware of how much he had aged. It was only after his death, when I printed these last photographs, that I saw for the first time a worn and weary look. He said that he was eighty-nine, when in fact he was almost ninety-two when he died.

162

Twenty years after I first traveled down it, the road to Taliesin West was straight and graveled. It ended at a new structure, a pylon that was like an open hand greeting visitors while at the same time it taught the desert manners, by pushing it back.

The airy canvas roofs
had been replaced by
sturdier materials, but
Taliesin West's distinc-   166
tive profile remained a   ■
landmark for me.   ■
                              ■
                              ■
                              ■

The drafting room in
1959 was the busiest
in Mr. Wright's long
167   career, and many
■   projects were finished
■   only after his death.

■

■

■

On the last day of my visit in March 1959 Mr. Wright decided that he would like to have aerial views of Taliesin West, so he asked me to hire a helicopter. I discovered that a helicopter rented for $125 an hour, whereas a small plane cost only $14 an hour. Thinking that I was being wise and frugal, I tentatively hired the plane and reported to Mr. Wright. He rejected the plane, money or no money. What he wanted was a helicopter on the premises.

"Besides," he said, "what makes you think you aren't worth the difference?"

When the helicopter was on its way, I went to Mr. Wright's study to inform him and get my instructions. While he was telling me what direction would be the most advantageous, I interrupted and asked him whether it would not be better for all concerned if he came along. He could order me to photograph exactly what he wanted and not have to depend on what I chose to shoot.

"No," he said, "one of us should stay here."

I detected his mischievous delight that it was I who was risking my neck and not he.

"Oh, come on," I said. "The worst that can happen is that we will be killed. I can see the headlines in the paper now: 'P. Guerrero and Friend Killed in Copter Crash.' Come, do it for me."

With a twinkle in his eye and a low chortle he waved me off. The entire crowd that made up the Fellowship, including Mr. Wright with his hat and cane as usual, gathered east of the outer buildings to see the spectacle of the helicopter landing. Center stage was not going to be wasted on just me.

After I completed my assignment the helicopter dropped me off at Taliesin West. I had to fly back to New York City later that day and did not have time to speak with Mr. Wright again.

I had said my final goodbye.

FRANK LLOYD WRIGHT: THE LATER YEARS

1932	Taliesin Fellowship founded, Spring Green, Wisconsin; "An Autobiography" published
1935	Fallingwater, Mill Run, Pennsylvania
1935	Broadacre City model exhibited, New York, New York
1936	Hanna (Honeycomb) House, Palo Alto, California
1936	Jacobs House I, Madison, Wisconsin
1936–44	S.C. Johnson and Son Administration Building and Tower, Racine, Wisconsin
1937–39	Johnson House (Wingspread), Racine, Wisconsin
1937–59	Taliesin West, Scottsdale, Arizona
1938	Manson House, Wausau, Wisconsin
1938	Suntop Homes, Ardmore, Pennsylvania
1938–54	Florida Southern College, Lakeland, Florida
1939	Pew House, Madison, Wisconsin
1939	Pauson House, Phoenix, Arizona (burned 1941)
1939	Auldbrass Plantation, Yemassee, South Carolina
1939	Schwartz House, Two Rivers, Wisconsin
1939	Sturges House, Brentwood Heights, California
1939	Rosenbaum House, Florence, Alabama
1939	Goetsch-Winckler House, Okemos, Michigan
1939	Pope-Leighey House, Falls Church, Virginia
1940	Affleck House, Bloomfield Hills, Michigan
1940–46	Oboler Studio Retreat, Malibu, California
1943	"An Autobiography" (revised edition) published
1943–59	Guggenheim Museum, New York, New York
1944	Jacobs House II, Middleton, Wisconsin
1945	Walter House (Cedar Rock), Quasqueton, Iowa
1946	Unitarian Meeting House, Madison, Wisconsin
1947–48	Galesburg Country Homes, Galesburg, Michigan
1947–50	Parkwyn Village, Kalamazoo, Michigan
1947–51	Usonia Homes, Pleasantville, New York
1949	Walker House, Carmel, California

1948	Morris Gift Shop, San Francisco, California
1949	Walker House, Carmel, California
1949	Neils House, Minneapolis, Minnesota
1950	David Wright House, Phoenix, Arizona
1950	Schaberg House, Okemos, Michigan
1950	Palmer House, Ann Arbor, Michigan
1950	Zimmerman House, Manchester, New Hampshire
1951	Glore House, Lake Forest, Illinois
1952	Pieper House, Paradise Valley, Arizona
1952	Price Company Tower, Bartlesville, Oklahoma
1952	Hillside Playhouse, Spring Green, Wisconsin, rebuilt after fire
1952	Anderton Court Shops, Beverly Hills, California
1953	Usonian Exhibition House and Pavilion, New York, New York
1953	Robert Llewellyn Wright House, Bethesda, Maryland
1953	Price House, Bartlesville, Oklahoma
1954	Price House, Paradise Valley, Arizona
1954	Hoffman Auto Showroom remodeled, New York, New York
1954	Plaza Hotel Suite remodeled, New York, New York
1954	Exhibition Pavilion at Hollyhock House, Los Angeles, California
1954–59	Beth Sholom Synagogue, Elkins Park, Pennsylvania
1955	Taliesin Line created for Schumacher; furniture for Heritage-Henredon Furniture Company
1955	Rayward-Shepherd House (Tirranna), New Canaan, Connecticut
1955	Lovness Cottage, Stillwater, Minnesota
1955	Kalita Humphreys Theater, Dallas, Texas
1955	Kundert Medical Clinic, San Luis Obispo, California
1956	Annunciation Greek Orthodox Church, Wauwatosa, Wisconsin
1956	Wyoming Valley Grammar School, Wyoming Valley, Wisconsin
1956	Marshall Erdman Company Prefab Homes
1957–62	Marin County Civic Center, San Rafael, California
1959–64	Grady Gammage Memorial Auditorium, Arizona State University, Tempe, Arizona
1959	Wright (born June 8, 1867) dies, April 9, Phoenix, Arizona; buried at Unity Chapel, Spring Green, Wisconsin

INDEX